Editor-in-Chief and Founder:
  *Lyndon H. LaRouche, Jr.*
Editorial Board: *Lyndon H. LaRouche, Jr. , Helga
  Zepp-LaRouche, Robert Ingraham, Tony
  Papert, Gerald Rose, Dennis Small, Jeffrey
  Steinberg, William Wertz*
Co-Editors: *Robert Ingraham, Tony Papert*
Technology: *Marsha Freeman*
Transcriptions: *Katherine Notley*
Ebooks: *Richard Burden*
Graphics: *Alan Yue*
Photos: *Stuart Lewis*
Circulation Manager: *Stanley Ezrol*

INTELLIGENCE DIRECTORS
Economics: *Marcia Merry Baker, Paul Gallagher*
History: *Anton Chaitkin*
Ibero-America: *Dennis Small*
Russia and Eastern Europe: *Rachel Douglas*
United States: *Debra Freeman*

INTERNATIONAL BUREAUS
Bogotá: *Miriam Redondo*
Berlin: *Rainer Apel*
Copenhagen: *Tom Gillesberg*
Lima: *Sara Madueño*
Melbourne: *Robert Barwick*
Mexico City: *Gerardo Castilleja Chávez*
New Delhi: *Ramtanu Maitra*
Paris: *Christine Bierre*
Stockholm: *Ulf Sandmark*
United Nations, N.Y.C.: *Leni Rubinstein*
Washington, D.C.: *William Jones*
Wiesbaden: *Göran Haglund*

ON THE WEB
e-mail: eirns@larouchepub.com
www.larouchepub.com
www.executiveintelligencereview.com
www.larouchepub.com/eiw
Webmaster: *John Sigerson*
Assistant Webmaster: *George Hollis*
Editor, Arabic-language edition: *Hussein Askary*

EIR (ISSN 0273-6314) *is published weekly
(50 issues), by EIR News Service, Inc.,
P.O. Box 17390, Washington, D.C. 20041-0390.
(703) 297-8434*

**European Headquarters:** E.I.R. GmbH, Postfach
Bahnstrasse 9a, D-65205, Wiesbaden, Germany
Tel: 49-611-73650
Homepage: http://www.eir.de
e-mail: info@eir.de
Director: Georg Neudecker

**Montreal, Canada:** 514-461-1557
eir@eircanada.ca

**Denmark:** EIR - Danmark, Sankt Knuds Vej 11,
basement left, DK-1903 Frederiksberg, Denmark.
Tel.: +45 35 43 60 40, Fax: +45 35 43 87 57. e-mail:
eirdk@hotmail.com.

**Mexico City:** EIR, Sor Juana Inés de la Cruz 242-2
Col. Agricultura C.P. 11360
Delegación M. Hidalgo, México D.F.
Tel. (5525) 5318-2301
eirmexico@gmail.com



**Postmaster:** Send all address changes to *EIR*, P.O.
Box 17390, Washington, D.C. 20041-0390.

Signed articles in *EIR* represent the views of the authors,
and not necessarily those of the Editorial Board.

# The 2018 Election:
# The Great Opportunity
# of this Century

# EIR Contents

www.larouchepub.com  Volume 45, Number 39, September 28, 2018

ZEPP-LAROUCHE WEBCAST

# Victory Over the Desperate British Empire Is Now Within Reach!

*This is the edited transcript of the Schiller Institute's September 20, 2018 New Paradigm interview with Helga Zepp-LaRouche by Harley Schlanger. A video of the webcast is available.*

**Harley Schlanger:** Hello, I'm Harley Schlanger from the Schiller Institute. Welcome to this week's webcast, featuring our founder, Helga Zepp-LaRouche.

There have been a few bombshells in the last couple of days that are shaping a new potential for the strategic situation, especially a potential for defeating the coup in the United States, with President Trump's order for document declassification. Helga, I think it's important that we start with that, because it does conform to what we've been calling for—the declassification of the whole story of who's behind this coup attempt and why. Why don't you catch us up with that?

**Helga Zepp-LaRouche:** Yes. I think this is the most important strategic development, because as we have said many times, while countries in the world are moving toward a completely new set of international relations, expressed in the New Silk Road and in win-win cooperation, it is also clear that it all depends on the United States. Depending on how the internal situation in the United States develops, I think it's a question of war and peace.

Two weeks ago, I mentioned Willy Wimmer's statement—which I agree with—that the only thing standing between all of us and World War III is the person of Donald Trump. That is not a full endorsement of Trump,

it's just the reality that the people who have been engaged in a coup attempt against him, together with the British government and British intelligence, these are the war-mongers and these are the people who are pushing for complete confrontation with Russia and China.

**Trump Orders Documents Declassified**

In this strategic context, it is super-important now, less than seven weeks before the midterm elections, that President Trump did, indeed, order the declassifi-

Senate Democrats/Flickr    Gage Skidmore    Senate Intelligence Committee    Senate Democrats/Flickr

*Democratic Party leaders are attempting to block the President's order to declassify documents pertaining to FISA court warrants. Shown are Sen. Chuck Schumer (left), Rep. Nancy Pelosi (center left), Sen. Mark Warner (center right), and Rep. Adam Schiff (right).*

cation of a lot of documents pertaining to the FISA Court warrants, all of which were based on the circulation of the fraudulent Steele dossier, a real intelligence operation; and also a lot of the emails, and interviews with 70 individuals involved in this affair.

While this is not yet public, it will be public, and basically we have to wait until they process all of this information and it gets out. It is very clear, from the reaction of the culprits, that, really, Trump has hit a raw nerve. You have a completely hysterical reaction from the leaders of the Democratic Party—Nancy Pelosi, Chuck Schumer, Adam Schiff, Mark Warner, others—who are saying that "under no circumstances must this information be declassified. This is risking the lives of sources" and whatnot. Pelosi and all the former heads of intelligence are coming out to scream and yell.

They all admit that President Trump does have the authority to do this. Then all these crimes will come out in the open, and the role of British intelligence will be absolutely crystal clear: there was no Russia collusion, but there was, indeed, criminal collusion between the Democratic Party apparatus, the heads of intelligence from the Obama Administration, and a foreign power, namely, Great Britain.

I think Trump is absolutely correct to say that this document declassification is going to be one of the proudest accomplishments of his Presidency, because this whole apparatus was a cancer which has been damaging the United States for a very long time.

So this is big. And I find it really scandalous that something which very well could be the biggest scandal in the history of the United States, is not being reported widely by the international media. When they report it, it's twisted and has a spin, and normal people who don't follow this in depth have no way of understanding the significance of this. I know that this is not so in the United States, but for example, the German media, I was really looking, and they hardly have anything about it at all—which tells you something, that it's not just fake news that they report, it's especially the suppression of really big stories, which is how they try to manipulate the population. So President Trump's decision to declassify the documents is big.

**Schlanger:** Helga, even in the United States, after the first day, the coverage fell off dramatically, relative to the importance of this. *The Hill* ran an interview with Trump, in which he commented on the greatest scandal, but I think it's also worth noting that the Pelosi, Schumer, Warner, and Schiff letter was essentially an appeal to the intelligence community, the Justice Department and the FBI, to defy Trump's order, creating a potential constitutional crisis.

Now, the other part of this, is that LaRouche PAC has for a long time demanded declassifying the other part—the British documents, the emails, the communications between the British and people like Brennan

and Clapper and others. So I think this is the other shoe that still has to drop.

**Papadopoulos Spills the Beans**

**Zepp-LaRouche:** Yes. But I think the first shoe is already dropping, or has already dropped, and I find it quite interesting that, of all people, George Papadopoulos—supposedly the one who triggered this whole investigation while drunk in a London bar, by mentioning that there was Russian hacking of the Democratic computers—two days ago, he gave a lengthy interview on Fox TV which I would advise all of you, our viewers and listeners, to make the effort and listen to it, because it's really revealing.

In that interview he said he was set up, that he was lured into this by a combination of Australian, British, Turkish and American intelligence; that he was entrapped in this, and he's now spilling the beans. He says it is the British, it's the Australians, which, by the way, is more or less the same thing because of the Five Eyes connection among those Commonwealth countries. Papadopoulos is saying this was all a setup, and it was the British.

This is really important and people should really listen to it, because this was, as far as I know, one of the so-called pretexts for the whole scandal to erupt, and now he is turning around saying he was set up, and was lured into this.

If this continues to happen, I think we are going to see more things. All the congressmen who have been looking into all of this have said that if the American people were able to know the extent of this crime, they would get really upset. I think this could be the big catharsis in American history.

**Schlanger:** This is so crucial, given the strategic developments that are occurring, that were the President freed from this yoke around his neck, this constant attack on him, there'd be potential for the United States to engage in collaboration, as you've been calling for, with the Chinese, the Russians, the Indians, the Japanese, for moving to a completely new economic system. We see this with the continuation of the "Singapore model" in the meetings this week between President Moon Jae-in of South Korea and North Korea's leader Kim Jong-un. This is a big step forward, isn't it?

## Moon and Kim Meet

**Zepp-LaRouche:** Oh yes. And it also shows, again, how idiotic those people were, who said that this was a big bluff and nothing would come of it. Because President Moon is now in Pyongyang for three days. As Moon and Kim travelled by open car through Pyongyang, they were greeted by thousands of people along their route. Many had unification flags.

Moon and Kim said they want to have complete agreement for a peace treaty by the end of the year, and big economic projects are on the horizon, which can be implemented the moment the sanctions stop. And I think it's also extremely important that this is part of the New Silk Road. In the province of Liaoning, the southernmost province in Manchuria, adjacent to North Korea, the government announced that it wants to integrate into its economic planning the extension of high-speed trains into North Korea all the way to Busan in the southern tip of South Korea, and in that way to fully integrate the Korean Peninsula into the Belt and Road Initiative.

That is exactly why there is such a strong hope that the promise—also made by President Trump, that he wants North Korea to become a prosperous country—is on a very good track.

So I think this is really important. The Schiller Institute, and I personally, have lived through all the trials of German unification, and therefore, I can vividly imagine what is going on in the hearts and minds of Koreans.

Families are coming together for the first time in many years, and people are just very happy. I remember that in 1989, Germans, for a certain period, were absolutely jubilant, and, indeed, were a better people. Unfortunately, as we have said many times, that historical chance was missed, because of the geostrategic efforts

Korea Summit Press Pool

*North Korean leader Kim Jong-un (left) and South Korean President Moon Jae-in, greet each other in the Demilitarized Zone, April 27, 2018.*

to dismantle the former Comecon economy, so the potential was not fully developed. You have many beautiful cities in East Germany now that they are fully restored, but you have an aging population, because people left Germany because economic development did not really take place in the way it could have, had the Eurasian Land-Bridge proposal we made at the time been fulfilled.

The situation is completely different with North and South Korea, because you have the Belt and Road Initiative, and therefore, I think this is really one of the great developments of our time.

## Putin and Erdogan Outflank in Idlib

**Schlanger:** That is a huge difference, because it's something that North Korea can be plugged into very quickly. The Chinese want to do it. The South Koreans want to do it. And it brings the whole Korean Peninsula that much closer to Europe.

The other situation that's evolving—and it's quite complicated—is that around Idlib province in Syria. On our Sept. 6 webcast we talked about Nikki Haley and John Bolton threatening Russia and Syria over an alleged, planned use by the Syrian Arab Army of chemical weapons, the civilian slaughter that was allegedly about to take place. It does appear that as a result of the summit between Presidents Putin and Erdogan that fake scenario has been outflanked. What's the latest that you have on the situation in Syria and in Idlib province?

**Zepp-LaRouche:** In the face of this absolutely pre-

*Russian President Vladimir Putin (left) and Turkish President Recep Tayyip Erdogan, shown at a press conference in Ankara, Turkey, April 3, 2018.*

programmed provocation, the Russian government provided the Organization for the Prohibition of Chemical Weapons, the U.S. State Department, and other governments with information and proof that the White Helmets had kidnapped children in order to have them appear as "victims" for the so-called chemical attack by Assad, thus constituting a completely false-flag operation. All the warmongers in the West, including U.S. National Security Advisor John Bolton, German Defense Minister Ursula von der Leyen, and all kinds of similarly-minded people, were already saying, "If there is a chemical attack by Assad, we will immediately have a military strike, which will be much more severe than the previous two." It definitely was a very good flank to interrupt the escalation of this operation, which could have gone completely out of control.

Now, in parenthesis, people should just reflect: What motive could Assad possibly have, when he has almost liberated, with the help of Russia, the entire territory of Syria, except for this little province of Idlib, to risk using chemical weapons? The Syrian government's chemical weapons were all destroyed, by the way, with international supervision, several years ago. Assad has no chemical weapons. Even if he still had some, why would he use them, given this scenario and this orchestration? It just doesn't make sense; it's a complete fabrication.

But it was a very serious development. President Putin and President Erdogan decided to outflank all this that by declaring a demilitarized zone of about 15-20 square kilometers that Russia and Turkey will enforce. It's not entirely clear how they're going to do it, be-

cause there are between 40-60,000 terrorists of various kinds—Al-Qaeda, ISIS, Al-Nusra, and their follower organizations in Idlib—and about 3 million civilians living in the province, so it obviously is a tedious and dangerous effort. But if the Turkish and Russian military forces work together, and with Russia having control of the airspace over this province, I think it can be done. I don't know exactly what the modalities are going to be, but I think this tactic has definitely derailed an otherwise extremely dangerous escalation. We just have to see how the situation evolves.

## Trade War, or New Bretton Woods?

**Schlanger:** Another area where there's escalation, is the imposition of new tariffs between the United States and China. It appears to be evolving into a real, full-fledged trade war. There's so much in the media attacking China, blaming China. Now there are reports that China's economy is "staggered" by this. What's the picture that you have on this situation, Helga?

**Zepp-LaRouche:** I think it's really unfortunate, because, you know, President Trump was on such a good track with President Xi Jinping. They had a very good state visit at Mar-a-Lago in April a year ago; then you had the "State visit-plus" of Trump and Melania in Beijing at the end of last year—this was all going in an absolutely good direction. But you have these people in the Trump Administration who are really China haters, like Peter Navarro, and also Larry Kudlow. Kudlow said that the initial implementation of these sanctions has "smashed" the Chinese economy already, which I think is absolutely far from being true. And Commerce Secretary Wilbur Ross said that the Chinese have "run out of bullets" already, which is really stupid.

Meanwhile, Trump announced a new round of tariffs of 10% on $200 billion worth of mostly consumer item imports from China, to go into effect Sept. 24, but increasing to 25% by the beginning of next year, should there be no deal by then. China does not import from the United States and the United States imports from China, so China cannot totally answer with a similar amount in terms of tariffs. But to think that China, if this thing escalates, has no other means to respond, is just completely foolish. After all, they have $1.3 trillion worth of U.S. securities as foreign exchange reserves; they could lower the value of their currency, for example, and undo the effect of all of these sanctions.

If you get into this kind of dynamic, however, it is really bad. It has absolutely nothing to do with the American System of economics. I think Trump means well, that he wants to bring industries back to the United States, but as we have said many times, in order to pull the world out of danger of a new financial crash much worse than that of 2008, we need a New Bretton Woods system; and this can only be done if the four most important powers come together—maybe more than four, but this is the core group which is absolutely necessary—namely the United States, Russia, China, and India, and possibly such countries as Japan. You cannot make enemies with the very countries you need for a New Bretton Woods system! I think trade war with China is really the wrong way to go.

I think the future lies with the New Paradigm: the participation of the United States in the New Silk Road, allowing American companies to invest in all the countries of the Belt and Road Initiative; allowing Chinese investments inside the United States, for example, in the renewal of infrastructure, and in the technological increase of productivity, such as joint cooperation for fusion power, joint space exploration—activities that dramatically increase the productivity of the economy, therefore making the cake bigger, not redistributing pieces of an ever-shrinking cake.

This is very unfortunate, and we will just increase our campaign to try to get a different debate going, namely one on a New Bretton Woods system, and joint ventures in third countries, because that discussion would bring a much, much better result. In the context of the danger of a financial crash, trade war is really not the way to go.

### Will the EU Collapse?

**Schlanger:** We're seeing quite a bit of activity in Europe right now. I'll pick out just three cases: The situation in Germany continues to be unstable. The coalition government is again in trouble. But then, we see useful and positive initiatives coming out of Italy and Austria. What's going to happen here? The German situation is especially troubling, because Germany could play such an important role, and yet you see such crazy things as, finally, someone coming out against Bundestag President Wolfgang Schäuble's "black zero" austerity policy, but for the wrong reason—so there can

be a German military buildup! How do we deal with this situation in Europe, Helga?

**Zepp-LaRouche:** I think former Foreign Minister Sigmar Gabriel basically said it: It just needs one more blow and the whole European Union could fall apart. I think that is absolutely true.

The effort to stick to geopolitics is not working. German diplomat Wolfgang Ischinger's statement to get rid of the "black zero," in order to have a military buildup, is just one example. Another example is that the EU has just decided that it wants to counter the Belt and Road Initiative, the New Silk Road.

Federica Mogherini, the so-called foreign minister of the EU, claims she has just travelled through 20 countries and they all would like European connectivity much better than working with China—which I *really* doubt! I don't know which countries she visited, maybe some countries on the Moon, or some asteroid, I don't know. But this just does not make any sense. I know what important governments are thinking, and they all tend to agree, except those under complete geopolitical control of the EU for one reason or another. They all agree that they have a much better opportunity when dealing with China, because of China's win-win cooperation approach.

Sticking to geopolitics is really not good. But this is not the only dynamic at work in Europe, because, as you mentioned, Italy, in spite of being blasted by the EU, by the European Central Bank, by ECB President Mario Draghi, by EU Commission President Jean-Claude Juncker, by all kinds of so-called "Europeans," is doing the right thing! Italian Undersecretary of State for Economic Development Michele Geraci was just at the G-20 Commerce Ministers meeting in Argentina, where he proposed reforming the World Trade Organization to make it fairer to every participating nation. Finance Minister Giovanni Tria was just in China working out a memorandum of understanding for joint cooperation, not only involving China and Italy in joint projects in the development of Africa—which is absolutely the way to go—but also intensifying cooperation between Alitalia and Chinese airline companies. So this is very good.

In Austria, Chancellor Sebastian Kurz has called for a forum to discuss the migrant crisis. He wanted to have an EU-African Union summit before the end of the year, when Austria must give up its presidency of the EU, but the EU refused! They don't want to discuss an overall orientation to the migrant crisis, but instead

*Russian President Vladimir Putin (left) and Austrian Chancellor Sebastian Kurz, shown at a press conference in Vienna, Austria, June 5, 2018.*



insist on just discussing the particulars of it. Just as have all the North African countries—Tunisia, Algeria, Morocco—the EU has refused to situate refugee camps on its soil for very good reasons.

So the EU policy is not functioning, and therefore, what Chancellor Kurz wants to do is much better. Since the EU refused to entertain a summit on the issue, Kurz will now hold an EU Africa *forum*, not for EU bureaucrats, but instead he is inviting leading European businessmen and firms to discuss industrial investment in Africa. That is much, much, much better.

So you have no unity in the European Union, as you mentioned. The German government is again in a major coalition crisis, because the coalition partners made this crazy deal to kick out Hans-Georg Maassen, the head of the internal agency for the protection of the Constitution (BfV)—it's roughly the equivalent of the FBI. He got caught in a bunch of stupid statements and lies, and so he was kicked out of that position, but they kicked him upstairs to make him Deputy Minister of the Interior under Horst Seehofer, which means he gets a lot more money. And people are really upset. Now, it's clear the SPD was involved in making this deal, so therefore they are now all protesting this and saying this is outrageous—it's just a phony theater, because everybody knows SPD head Andrea Nahles must have been involved in making this deal.

I don't know what will come of this coalition, but they're all suffering from an inability to correct the mistakes of their policy. That you have such a strong populist—or right-wing, or worse than right-wing—movement now in Germany in the form of the Alternative für Deutschland, is the result of wrong economic policies.

It's not just that many people oppose the migrants; it's because they feel economically sidelined and have suffered only disadvantages from the policy of the "black zero," and globalization.

The German government is clearly unable to reflect on why all of this is happening. I don't think this is the end of it: I think all of this means that European nations are drifting further apart. There is a way out, however, and that is cooperation with China in the development of Africa.

We will continue to propose it and produce reports proposing very concretely how it can be done.

## Make History with the Schiller Institute!

**Schlanger:** Helga, we're basically out of time. I want to take a moment, however, to congratulate you on the extraordinary conference you presided over in New York City last week [see *Executive Intelligence Review*, Sept. 21, 2018 for conference texts], which people can see in the videos on the Schiller Institute website, Panel I and Panel II, where the process, the motion toward pulling together a Four Power agreement for a New Bretton Woods, was put forward very effectively by people from all over the world.

I encourage our viewers to go to our website, look at these videos, and join. Become a member of the Schiller Institute so we can bring the West out of this insane British policy of geopolitics and into this New Paradigm.

Helga, is there anything you want to add to that?

**Zepp-LaRouche:** I ask you, our viewers, to sign our Petition for a New Bretton Woods. We will publish this now: We have many VIP signatures, and also an increasing number of just normal citizens, and we will circulate this petition at the UN General Assembly this month to try to influence the discussion for a new financial system, a new credit system—rather, a New Bretton Woods system. So, sign the petition, and get it around as widely as possible, and share the view of this webcast, to build up the viewership. As you may have noticed, we are discussing here things which are absolutely not in the mainstream media, but are nevertheless extremely important for people to know.

**Schlanger:** OK. People can work on building up the audience for next week. Helga, we'll see you again next week.

**Zepp-LaRouche:** I hope so!

# Reality Now Intrudes on the Anti-Trump Propagandists—How About You?

by Barbara Boyd

Radio Free Europe/
Radio Liberty

*This is an edited transcript of a presentation by Barbara Boyd to Lyndon LaRouche's Manhattan Project Town Hall Meeting, Sept. 22, 2018. Boyd is the author of the LaRouche PAC investigative report, "Robert Mueller is an Amoral Legal Assassin: He Will Do His Job If You Let Him."*

I am not going to give you an extended, factual presentation. Today, we really do stand on the precipice of a fundamental change. With Trump's order to declassify the documents—which we've long sought to have declassified—this battle against the coup in the United States which we've been fighting has entered a truly new phase.

Today, I want to draw out certain ideas we already know. Mostly I want to talk to you about how propaganda works, because I think it's essential that people think about this in some depth.

## Tour de Coup

Let's just take, for example, the coup events of the past month. Let's think about them not from the standpoint of a consumer of news, or you just sitting there being hit with this stuff. Rather, just for a second, put yourself in the shoes of the enemy propagandist, who is intent on overturning the results of the 2016 election,

with Donald Trump as the target. Let's look at the series of images which have been presented to you. Let's get inside their minds, put yourself in the meetings of the Washington, D.C. and London PR shops that make a business out of this. I know, it's like taking a swim down at the sewage treatment plant, but bear with me, because I just need you to think this through a little bit.

First, we have the death of John McCain. Powerful themes hit you endlessly, just preceding his death and through his very public funeral: war hero, jovial rascal, iconoclast, father, cancer victim—just like Ted Kennedy; steadfast champion of the postwar order which allegedly kept world peace. Endless soldiers and ordinary citizens salute his casket as the hearse rides by. This image meant something when it was the train carrying Bobby Kennedy's body, but it has now been staged endlessly to honor every single one of the Establishment's heroes. In the midst of this, Senator McCain is serenaded by Barack Obama and George W. Bush. Donald Trump, according to this propaganda campaign, sits in the White House fuming and spewing out hatred.

Then we have Bob Woodward's new book, *Fear.* Donald Trump is here portrayed as an enraged infant, throwing (pardon my language) shit at every turn against the beliefs we allegedly hold dear. For example the war in Afghanistan, globalization, the FBI/Department of Justice as an entity wholly independent from the President, our alliances which have allegedly kept the world safe from war. We can talk endlessly about how Woodward makes all of this up, but that kind of misses the purloined letter principle of Edgar Allan Poe, which sits right there in the middle of the book for everybody to see. All the stuff that Trump allegedly tramples on are things the Establishment holds most dear—their present, post-Roosevelt, British fascist order, elaborated at great length by Bob Woodward.

Then we have the Brett Kavanaugh theatre and "me-too." The bet here is that the Women's March hysteria, which had its dry run back in the day before Trump was inaugurated, can now be repeated to mobilize the Democratic Party suburban female vote for the mid-term elections. More than that though, it intersects the coup: We see male Senator after male Senator proclaiming that there is no presumption of innocence, that neither the accuser nor Brett Kavanaugh actually needs to be heard by anyone, to decide what amounts to a charge of criminal assault. Note, she is the person to be believed—totally, completely, and without further examination. There is a secondary goal to the Kavanaugh business, namely, creating the lawless and emotion- and rage-driven atmosphere which would have to accompany and does accompany any putative impeachment of the current President.

Then we have the most recent foray of the *New York Times*, the one which occurred last night. Based on the *Times'* profile of Donald Trump, which they themselves have created, they believe that the revelation that Rod Rosenstein had discussed mobilizing the cabinet to use the 25th Amendment to the Constitution to get rid of Trump—and, right after James Comey was fired, had discussed wearing a wire himself to record the President in the White House—would result in the President

## I Am Part of the Resistance Inside the Trump Administration

I work for the president but like-minded colleagues and I have vowed to thwart parts of his agenda and his worst inclinations.

Sept. 5, 2018

*Leer en español 阅读简体中文版 閱讀繁體中文版 한국어로 읽기 日本語で読む*



*Rod Rosenstein, Deputy Attorney General.*

*"Resist" op-ed in the New York Times.*

shooting from the hip and firing Rosenstein. Rosenstein should have been disqualified a long, long time ago from any participation in the Mueller investigation, if indeed, we were functioning under anything other than a lawless regime.

The propagandists believed that this revelation would set off the constitutional crisis they have long sought as the atmosphere for removing the duly-elected President. The propagandists themselves suggested that whoever leaked this just might be the same person who wrote the anonymous piece in the *New York Times* that accompanied the pumping of Woodward's book, which again painted an administration in chaotic disarray being subverted from within, in the midst of a coup.

### Are You Profiled?

None of the things which these propagandists write are, of course, true in any respect. Rather, they are based on themes they think will stick, based on how they think *you* think. And *you*, my dear audience, not the President, are the real targets of this coup. If the coup succeeds, we're back in the days of Bush and Obama. We're back in the days of clinging to an empire in decline. We're back in the days of facing the almost certain inevitability of nuclear annihilation, the modern form, as they would express it, of the quip anticipating

# Trump Orders Declassification Of FBI Documents Sought By House Republicans

September 17, 2018 · 6:48 PM ET

MARTINA STEWART

Carter Page, former foreign policy adviser for the Trump campaign, speaks to the media after testifying before the House Intelligence committee on Nov. 2, 2017.

Mark Wilson/Getty Images

the French Revolution, *après moi, le déluge.* We're back in the days in which entertainment and pornography replace scientific thought and poetry; in which drugs and rage replace bold ideas and the serenity necessary for truly creative thought.

So, unless you think about *how* you think, and whether you have the courage to think boldly and break out of your habits to contemplate big and fundamental conceptions of mankind and nature, they will have snared you, based on *what* you think now They think you cannot change, that you'll stick to your habits locked in fear, that you'll stick to our present paradigm, just as they have profiled you, just as they themselves are stuck.

Two monumental events interrupted this crafted and evolving propaganda scenario in the last week, now that reality has intruded. First, the President

White House/Pete Souza

*President Barack Obama (left) gets a briefing from one of his men, John Brennan, then Assistant to the President for Homeland Security, Dec. 14, 2012.*

moved—as we have long called for—to declassify certain foundational documents in the coup itself. The Carter Page fourth FISA warrant application; the text messages of key figures in the Justice Department, including James Comey; the FD-302s involving Bruce Ohr and the FBI.

Second, George Papadopoulos. If you recall him, he's the young Trump volunteer who suffered an endless series of entrapments on British soil, entrapments which actually involved collaboration between British intelligence, Barack Obama and John Brennan, set up to feed the FBI a fabricated story to create the contextual basis for investigating the President. This week, Papadopoulos, facing a sentence of only a month in prison at this point, began to describe the early phases of the British-orchestrated coup against Trump as he experienced it personally, beginning in April of 2016.

With these two events, the British have completely freaked out. According to the President's own account, they complained heatedly. So, in all probability, did the entirety of his intelligence community. So, in all probability, did certain media figures—the trusted ones who have been the proud recipients of the drip, drip, drip torture of propaganda against the President. So did the compromised Gang of Eight in the Congress—the designated members of Congress who hear the intelligence community's various insane versions of reality on a weekly basis.

You see, if this stuff comes out and is understood in all its implications by the American people, the coup is over. The people will fully understand that a foreign power, the British, acting in a conspiracy with a sitting President, Barack Obama, fabricated evidence against

DIA /Staff Sgt. Jonathan Lovelady

*Left to right: James Comey, FBI Director, John Brennan, CIA Director, and James Clapper, Director of National Intelligence, present their global threat assessments to the House Permanent Select Committee on Intelligence in Washington, D.C. on Feb. 4, 2014.*

the President's political rival, a candidate for President of the United States, Donald Trump. First, they tried to destroy Trump's candidacy by painting him with the Russian agent brush; then they proceeded to try to destroy his Presidency by adding to the palette "sex freak," "infantile man-child," "savage racist," "misogynist"—all the stuff you hear repeatedly.

When these documents come out, people will go to jail. The entirety of the corporate news media will go belly up. The professional class will have to just shut up and re-educate itself about our Constitutional and fundamental human values. And, I might add, Lyndon LaRouche will be exonerated. That is, if—and only if—our organization tells the story. Because we are really the only ones who can get this right, based on the vast library of knowledge Lyn has bequeathed to us to get this exactly right.

### 'Submissive Void of an Uninformed Public'

As with Trump, the British demanded LaRouche's head. As with Trump, they proceeded under a "counter-intelligence" secret rubric to surveil and fabricate evidence. In LaRouche's case, it was not under FISA, but under Executive Order 12333. As with Trump, they proceeded with a blunderbuss and illegal prosecution in which extant legal rules and precedents were completely abandoned, and associates of LaRouche stared at jail sentences lasting decades if they stuck with him and refused to become Judases.

The President has it somewhat right when he describes himself as a "stable genius." That is, an agent of fundamental change. That is the type of person the British and their imperial predecessors target for absolute destruction. LaRouche, of course, is a much better and more able, stable genius because he acted to constantly expand his field of knowledge; he drove himself to make breakthrough after breakthrough in knowledge of the human mind and the physical universe; he acted on the principle of constant and progressive change—the enemy of any fixed social arrangement such as the present British Empire.

It is no accident that in the hideous National Defense Authorization Act, written by Obama holdovers but adopted by the neo-liberals and neo-conservatives who are seeking to subvert Trump, China and Russia are designated as "revisionist powers," and we are told that that is what makes them our enemies. If you look up what "revisionist" means in this context, you will find that it means that they seek to "change the present order." Change—the fundamental law of the actual universe, by anyone's accurate epistemology. "That's our enemy," according to them. Think about that.

So, the battle is joined. As opposed to the propagandists who endlessly plough the President for flaws and present him in ways to ignite American's most stupid and fixed passions, we can now make clear to people exactly what has happened to them over the last two decades. It is the British Empire, a modern feudal empire based on controlling the world's monetary supply, rather than the landed aristocracy of old. It is an empire that conducts its wars through propaganda, through its ability to manipulate popular opinion and the popular mind. Its warfare goals were long ago set forth by Bertrand Russell—that is, convincing a labile population that snow is actually black.

John Pilger wrote a very good article in *Consortium News* recently, entitled "Hold the Front Page: The Reporters Are Missing," which I recommend to you concerning the operations of the Empire. In it, he notes that in the 1970s he met Leni Riefenstahl, Hitler's filmmaker, "whose propaganda mesmerized the German public." According to Pilger, "She told me that the messages of her films were dependent not on 'orders from above' but on the submissive void of an uninformed public. 'Did that include the liberal educated bourgeoisie?' I asked. 'Everyone,' she said. Propaganda always wins if you allow it."

## Our Role

Our role here is not to meet lies with lies, but to present the truth and goad the population out of its fixed views and deadly preoccupations. We are aided by the tremendous progress being made in the world—the big and bold ideas encompassed in the Belt and Road, but otherwise presented in the most unvarnished form by *this* political movement. We are at the point where the enemy is clear to us and we can tell its story to its detriment. We are at the point where we can provide this great population with a real vision and, most fundamentally, real hope for the future. Among our most devastating weapons are music and poetry—the means to elevate and stimulate the human mind to live outside of its own perceived limitations, that is, to change.

For example, I have been thinking a lot recently about Shelley's poem, the "Mask of Anarchy." It is considered to be the greatest political poem ever written in the English language. It speaks of Empire based on the slaughter of peaceful protesters in Manchester, England by the British oligarchy in Shelley's time. It paints a devastating picture and caricature of the people and traits involved in that slaughter—the oligarchs. For example, in thinking recently about Al Green, Kesha Rogers' opponent in Texas, I thought Shelley's description of fraud most apt. He says, as he lines up the allegorical traits which caused this massacre:

Portrait by Alfred Clint
*Percy Bysshe Shelley*

4.
Next came Fraud, and he had on,
Like Lord Eldon, an ermined gown;
His big tears, for he wept well,
Turned to mill-stones as they fell.

5.
And the little children, who
Round his feet played to and fro,
Thinking every tear a gem,
Had their brains knocked out by them.

What could be a more precise description of Al Green and the fate of the uneducated children who have been sucked in by the Resist movement? In his poem, Shelley moves from presenting his devastating caricature of the Empire, to that which will defeat it—the emboldened hope of a population educating itself and seeking, hungrily and aroused, justice itself, through, he says, science, and poetry, and thought. A population, I would add, whose thinking has been changed. The end of the poem has been cited widely all over the world many times:

91.
Rise like Lions after slumber
In unvanquishable number—
Shake your chains to earth like dew
Which in sleep had fallen on you—
Ye are many—they are few.

Now is not the time to do a full study of this poem, but, I would submit, it should very much be our anthem and theme in the present moment.

# Trump Declassification Order a Blow to Coup Behind Mueller Russiagate Fraud

by Harley Schlanger

Sept. 21—The order by President Donald Trump, on Sept. 17, to declassify documents related to the investigation of alleged Russian interference in the 2016 election campaign and Trump's "collusion" with Russia, is a bombshell escalation—significant and necessary—against the ongoing coup being run to destroy his presidency. When combined with the revelations in an interview that Fox News' Martha MacCallum did with George Papadopoulos the following day, we see evidence now being brought into the open which confirms what LaRouche PAC has charged from the beginning: That the charges against Russia and Trump are a fraud, a product of collusion between the Obama/Clinton intelligence team and the highest levels of British intelligence, in a desperate defense of the collapsing post-Cold War geopolitical order.

But, no sooner had the President finally acted to declassify foundational documents in the coup against him, than the British, and to a lesser extent the Australians began to shriek. According to the President, "some of our best allies" had problems with his order, for the reason that the coup was instigated because the British demanded Donald Trump's head, as far back as 2015, as this news service has documented. It was the British, not the Russians, who intervened into the 2016 U.S. elections and now they are panicked at being exposed, not only for their role in the election but for why they did it.

As of now, the President has sent the documents to Justice Department Inspector General Michael Horowitz for review, while making clear that the documents will come out. He said that expedition was the key test for him and others in getting these documents to the

American public. There is also a sitting grand jury in Washington, D.C. hearing evidence against former FBI Deputy Director Andrew McCabe and possibly others, concerning leaks to the media, false statements to those investigating leaks, and release of classified information.

These documents will show conclusively that those behind the coup attempt are "war mongers," as Helga Zepp-LaRouche described them in her Sept. 20 webcast, the same people "who are pushing for complete confrontation with Russia and China." For the sake of avoiding a downward spiral to possible nuclear con-

Marshall Center/U.S. Army
Sgt. Amanda Moncada
*Bruce Ohr*

FBI
*Peter Strzok*

frontation between the U.S. and Russia, the full story must be presented, and the real criminals of the British imperial order, sometimes misleadingly called the "Deep State," must be brought to trial.

## Trump's Declassification Bombshell

President Trump specified, in his order, that several sets of documents be declassified, and their contents be made available to the public. These include nineteen pages of the application to the FISA court for a warrant, which approved surveillance of Trump campaign operatives, beginning with volunteer Carter Page; FBI interviews in connection with the FISA applications; all FBI reports related to the FBI interview with Department of

Justice (DOJ) official Bruce Ohr, who remained in contact with discredited "former" British intelligence operative Christopher Steele, after the FBI officially severed its relationship with him; all text messages, emails, etc., relating to the Russian investigation, to and from former FBI Director James Comey, Deputy Director Andrew McCabe, Ohr, and leading FBI operatives Peter Strzok and Lisa Page.

Much is already known about what will be revealed by these documents. Most importantly, that there was an intent by the perpetrators, from the beginning of the "Never Trump" operation, to defeat Trump in the election, and, failing to do that, to use the Russiagate story as an "insurance policy," as disgraced FBI agent Peter Strzok texted to his mistress, FBI attorney Lisa Page. The fraudulent story of Russian hacking has been demolished by a special report of the Veteran Intelligence Professionals for Sanity and its technical expert, William Binney. Binney had been a top official of the National Security Agency (NSA) until he resigned after 9/11 and exposed the deliberate incompetence embedded in the NSA surveillance program, which prevented the intelligence community from forestalling the 9/11 attacks on our nation.

It is also known that Robert Mueller, as FBI Director after the 9/11 attacks, engaged in "aggressive deception" to cover up for the true authors of the attack, his masters running the British Empire. Strzok and Page—members of Mueller's team until they were dismissed after the release of some of their text messages by DOJ Inspector General Horowitz—admitted in the texts that though they could find no evidence of Russian interference or Trump collusion, they must keep digging, knowing they could shape an environment, through constant repetition of the lies, that would build the "Resist" movement to get rid of Trump.[1]

White House/Pete Souza

*John Brennan, Assistant to the President for Homeland Security, speaking with President Obama in the White House dining room, February 2010.*

*Carter Page*

Declassifying the documents specified by the President can now fill in the full picture of the treacherous collusion that actually took place—that there was never collusion by Trump with Russia, but between the neocon/neoliberal gang of Bush and Obama officials, and the actual authors of Russiagate operating within the secret web of British intelligence.

In comments made to *The Hill* newspaper on September 19, Trump defended his call for declassifying documents presented to the super-secret FISA Court because, in their application, the FBI "used Carter Page as a foil in order to surveil a candidate for the presidency of the United States." Trump said he believes that the FISA Court's judges may have been "misled" by the FBI. The full release, he added, will demonstrate that the whole investigation is "a hoax beyond a witch hunt … one of the greatest scandals in the history of our country." By releasing the documents, the public can decide for themselves what is true—"All I want to do is be transparent," he concluded.

Justice Department officials went four times to the FISA Court to obtain warrants to surveil Carter Page. The applications centered on "intelligence" provided by the discredited Steele dossier, used by the FBI despite its knowledge that the charges in it were false and that it was the product of "opposition research" paid for by the Clinton campaign through Fusion GPS—a crucial piece of the filing which was not communicated to the court. Among the staffers at Fusion GPS was Nellie Ohr, wife of DOJ official Bruce Ohr.

LaRouche PAC has called for a second round of declassification, that of all documents originating with British intelligence networks demanding an investigation of Trump and his campaign—including the secretive visit to Washington in early summer 2016 by Robert Hannigan, the former GCHQ chief. Hannigan delivered documents to then CIA Director John Brennan, alleging they had obtained suspicious electronic communications coming from Russian agents from the summer of 2015

---

1. See the LaRouche PAC Special Investigative Report into Russiagate by Barbara Boyd, published Sept. 27, 2017: https://larouchepac.com/20170927/robert-mueller-amoral-legal-assassin-he-will-do-his-job-if-you-let-him

who were preparing to interfere in the U.S. elections. These documents have been cited as providing the impetus for the creation of a "Get Trump" task force organized by Brennan, followed by the official convening of a task force under FBI Director Comey at the end of July, after Trump had secured the Republican Party nomination.

That Trump's actions have hit a raw nerve is clear from the reactions of leading Democrats, who denounced him in hysterical terms. Senators Chuck Schumer and Mark Warner joined with House leaders Nancy Pelosi and Adam Schiff to draft an open letter to DOJ officials, insisting that no action be taken until they, and their Republican counterparts in the Gang of Eight (party leaders of both Houses of Congress), have been briefed. Describing Trump's action as a "brazen abuse of power," their letter calls for officials to defy a presidential order.

Ranking Democratic members of the Oversight and Judiciary Committees, Elijah Cummings and Jerrold Nadler, called Trump's move "reckless and irresponsible," saying it is a "desperate attempt to distract" from special counsel/legal hitman Robert Mueller's investigation of Trump and his campaign. Rep. Eric Swalwell, another outspoken figure of the House Democratic "Get Trump" grouping, accused the President of being "absolutely lawless," and then issued a thinly veiled threat: "This is an abuse of power. His days of unchecked abuses are numbered."

For these Democrats, and former officials such as John Brennan—and the "mainstream" anti-Trump media, led by the *New York Times*, the *Washington Post* and CNN—the action to expose of the truth about the witch hunt is proof of Trump's collusion with Russia, and obstruction of justice! The *New York Times* contributed a lengthy piece of fiction, purporting to be an authoritative review, on September 21, under the title, "The Plot to Subvert an Election: Unraveling the Russia Story So Far"!

*Robert Hannigan, Director, GCHQ (2014-2017).*

## Papadopoulos Exposes the British

A second shoe dropped with unexpected revelations from George Papadopoulos in his interview with Fox News. Papadopoulos was a relatively unknown consultant appointed in 2016 to a Trump foreign policy advisory committee. According to his report to Fox interviewer MacCallum, he became the subject of an intense targeting campaign by individuals with British MI6 and CIA/FBI connections. When questioned by Mueller's team, he was charged with "lying" to the FBI. After entering a guilty plea, he was sentenced to a 14-day jail sentence.

The subject of his interrogation by Mueller's team was the allegation that he had been told by a "Russian," Joseph Mifsud, during a meeting on April 26, 2016, that the Russians had "dirt" on Hillary Clinton. Mifsud was actually a shadowy Maltese professor/diplomat with documented connections to the highest levels of British intelligence. Following this meeting, on May 10, as the story goes, he confided this to an Australian diplomat, Alexander Downer, during a drunken encounter in a London bar. Downer subsequently reported it to Australian officials, and it later got to the FBI. (Downer was the Australian High Commissioner to the UK and Australian intelligence is part of the "Five Eyes" coordinated intel network.) The FBI claims that Downer's report—that Papadopoulos told him about Russian hacking of Clinton campaign documents—is what led to the opening of the FBI investigation.

But in the interview with Fox, Papadopoulos' description of his meeting with Downer has the profile of a sting conducted by British intelligence and the CIA, to be fed into the FBI as pretext for the unprecedented FBI counterintelligence investigation of a Presidential election campaign. He told Fox that Downer and his accomplice, an Australian intelligence official, Erika Thompson, "were incredibly suspicious. It was clear this meeting [with Downer] was completely controlled, and was not a random invitation for a drink."

Papadopoulos asked, "Why was an Australian intelligence officer meeting with me and probing me about … what the campaign was doing in regard to Russia, in April, before Mifsud told me about the dirt?" He added, about the meeting, "I do not remember at all talking about e-mails with Downer. He himself has contradicted himself … at least three times…. What I remember was that he was incredibly belligerent, he despised Trump, he was very hostile toward the campaign."

MacCallum then showed a tweet from him: "The BRITISH (Stefan Halper), AUSTRALIANS (Alexander Downer and Erika Thompson) and TURKISH) … all spied on an American citizen and campaign. Obama, Brennan and Clapper knew." Asked to explain this tweet, he said, "I have never knowingly met a Russian official in my life. However, while I was in the campaign, I had an incredible amount of interactions with British diplomats." He added, "I have no idea why Stefan Halper lured me to London for the meeting, but it's impossible that the British had no idea about what was going on."

Halper, like Mifsud and Downer, has ties to both British intelligence and the FBI/CIA. Halper, who met with Papadopoulos in September 2016, also met with Carter Page in July 2016, speaking with both about Russian hacking—quite a coincidence!

When asked by the BBC on September 19 about Papadopoulos having identified him as a spy, Downer dodged the question, saying "I don't want this whole issue of Donald Trump and his team and the Russians and so on to interfere with Australia's relationship with the

UN/Paulo Filgueiras

*Alexander Downer, Australian High Commissioner to the U.K. (2014-2018).*

United States. It's a toxic issue." This, from the source credited by the FBI with providing the intelligence used to open the whole Russiagate investigation!

An additional FBI sting operation took place in May 2016, when a Russian going by the name Hank Greenberg met with Trump confidant and former adviser Roger Stone. Greenberg, who served as an FBI informant for 17 years, told Stone he could provide information from Russia on the Clintons, if Trump personally gave him $2 million. Stone rejected the offer. Stone has become a target of the Russiagate investigation, as Mueller's team insists he had advanced knowledge of the Russian "hack," through ties with Wikileaks and the hacker Guccifer. Stone denies this, and, as with every aspect of the investigation, no evidence to prove the allegations has been produced.

## Americans Must Act!

The Papadopoulos revelations, added to what will come out from a thorough review of the declassified documents, should substantially damage the "Get Trump" campaign. The revelations answer the question as to why Russiagate was launched in the first place, but the American people must actually demand an end to it. Shutting down the witch hunt will enable Trump to pursue his campaign promise to end useless and endless foreign wars and focus on the actual development of the United States and nation-to-nation collaboration on economic development. These wars, and the globalist financial system they support, were conducted on behalf of British geopolitical and financial objectives. This is what the British sponsors of Russiagate, and their American collaborators, are desperately trying to prevent.

*Stefan Halper, FBI informant.*

## INTERVIEW WITH KESHA ROGERS

# 'Stop Greedy Al Green's Impeachment Drive Against Trump'

*This is an edited transcript of an interview with Kesha Rogers, Independent candidate for U.S. Congress in the 9th CD in Texas. She was interviewed by* EIR *Co-Editor Tony Papert on Sunday, Sept. 23, 2018.*

**EIR:** We're on the phone with Kesha Rogers, who is on the Nov. 6 ballot as an Independent candidate for Congress in Texas' 9th Congressional District. Kesha, what are your reasons for running, and why an Independent campaign? Many people would think an Independent campaign would have to be purely symbolic.

EIRNS

*Kesha Rogers, Independent for U.S. Congress in the 9th CD in Texas.*

**Kesha Rogers:** I'm running in the 9th Congressional District of Texas to challenge and defeat incumbent Al Green. I am running as an Independent, even though I grew up as a Franklin Roosevelt Democrat—in the tradition of Franklin Roosevelt, fighting for the forgotten men and women of this nation. I ran two congressional campaigns, successful campaigns, to secure the nomination of the Democratic Party in 2010 and 2012, winning those nominations. And, as a Democrat, I forced a run-off election in 2014 on a platform of saving NASA and impeaching Obama. I took on that campaign fight because it became clear to me that the Democratic Party has become increasingly controlled by Wall Street and the warmongering interests that are for regime change wars and bailing out the financial interests of Wall Street,

moving away from the tradition of Franklin Roosevelt.

Unfortunately, this has now become the standard for the Democratic Party. But the deciding moment for me in leaving the Democratic Party came after the grotesque nomination process of Hillary Clinton and when I saw that she was clearly going to be a continuation of the Bush/Obama drive toward regime change and war, and would continue supporting the speculative interests of Wall Street.

In the 2016 election, a real shift occurred, in which the American people voted to elect a President, Donald Trump, who was making it very clear that he stood in opposition to the policies that had existed not only under the Obama Administration, but also under the Bush/Cheney Administration before.

We saw many blue-collar workers, Independents and even Democrats change over to vote for Donald Trump because he clearly enunciated his desire to go back to the productive standards of the United States. However, there continue to be forces within the Republican Party, also, which don't understand what those American System productive standards are. And that's why my campaign as an Independent is so important right now. And it's important because of the nature of this midterm election, campaigning nationally, going after the forces behind people like Al Green and others who stand with him, with their number-one objective being the impeachment of this constitutionally elected President.

## The American System, Not Wall Street

**EIR:** Do you want to tell us more about your background? I know you're pretty well known in your district and beyond.

**Rogers:** Sure. I have been, first of all, a student of the American System of political economy. I have campaigned for many years on the economic platform of bringing about growth and economic development through committing to an advanced science driver approach, restoring our high-technology manufacturing, and restoring our industry generally.

*Statue of Alexander Hamilton in New York City's Central Park.*



This has been a result of a 15-year association and friendship with a leading economist and scientist, Lyndon LaRouche, with whom you are very familiar. My growth and experience developed from being able to know Mr. LaRouche and study not only his breakthroughs in the science of physical economy, but also his enrichment of the ideas of our first Treasury Secretary, Alexander Hamilton. In his writings on economics, together with his role in the development of our Constitution, Hamilton established the essence of what the productive standard of a nation should be. That work has been advanced by the breakthroughs in the scientific and economic methods of Lyndon LaRouche.

In addition to my opposition to policies of war, regime change and geopolitics, a lot of my campaigns and my organizing over the many years now, has been the result of going out and fighting for legislation to reverse the continuing destruction of our economic process, where you've seen a collapse in the real economy, a collapse in job growth, in the commitment to scientific advancement. As a candidate for Congress, my number-one platform has always been to save NASA, and fully fund our space program as the economic driver or engine for real productive growth.

In my past campaigns, this really moved and transformed Texans and Americans, because they saw something in me different from what have been accepted as the left/right political norms. They saw in my campaign something different—a commitment to economic growth led by a science-driver, something not being presented by the establishment party factions.

As my campaign is unfolding, the institution of the Presidency is under total and continuous attack. One of the leaders of that attack is a leading money-making crony who sits on the Financial Services Committee in the House of Representatives—a man who has continued to support the policies of bailing out Wall Street, who has continued to support the policies of drug legalization, who has continued to support the war policy, and who is now campaigning on a one-note agenda: to impeach the President of the United States. He claims—publicly—that the President doesn't even have to commit a crime to be impeached! That's my opponent, Al Green.

Let me repeat that: Al Green—now being joined by Representatives Nancy Pelosi and Maxine Waters of California, and Jim Clyburn of North Carolina—has said that the President need not commit a crime in order to be impeached. No crime. None!

This is the standard that we're up against right now. The American people know that this is a complete hoax and a fraud, and that what such people represent is to the detriment of the entire nation.

## This May Be the Most Important Election

**EIR:** Do you want to say more about Al Green in the District?

**Rogers:** I have issued an Open Letter to the people of the 9th Congressional District, titled: "You Deserve a Better Future than Rep. Al 'Impeachment' Green Would Allow You." We have printed 20,000 copies, and we are circulating them throughout the District right now. We've been hitting businesses and going door to door in the community; the responses we're getting are quite overwhelming in support of our campaign against the hypocrisy and the insanity of Al Green.

For the more than twelve years that Congressman Green has been in Congress, many people have noticed that he is the "unseen Congressman." He has not

EIRNS/Marsha Bowen

*Campaigning for Kesha Rogers in Houston, Aug. 10, 2018.*

EIRNS/Bryan Barajas

*Rogers at the Houston Afro-Caribbean Praise Jam, Sept. 21, 2018.*

been around to care for his constituents.

Congressman Green just spoke to the Congressional Black Caucus on September 13, in a panel titled something like "Impeachment, a Necessary Remedy for Bigotry." Al Green did not go into the Congressional Black Caucus to discuss with them strategies for dealing with poverty, the unprecedented crime rate, drug trafficking and overdosing, human trafficking, and all the other things that are killing members of his constituency. No discussion about flood control, or infrastructure, or how to reverse the downward economic trend, while the people of this District are being driven deeper and deeper into economic despair. Instead, he strutted around, using the "race card" to attack the President, to avoid any discussion related to his responsibility to help the residents of his own District, my District.

More and more people in the District have come to recognize that we have a congressman who has not held a real town hall meeting—directly addressing his constituents—in years. It has become apparent that his concept of poverty alleviation is more of "how to make people a little bit more comfortable with their poverty," instead relieving them of it, of actually eradicating poverty.

This is something that people now see, and something they completely despise. People don't want handouts. They are looking for a *hand-up*, they're looking for ways to improve the economic conditions of their lives, and right now, we have a Congress member who

is either oblivious to this or simply doesn't give a damn.

This is the difference between him and me. There are many things in my Platform and my Open Letter that address precisely this. Over the past years, my Platform has focused on looking at the standards set by the Presidents who promoted real economic growth, such as John F. Kennedy. We are using the example of the space program as the great engine, the real economic driver in boosting the society, one that put millions to work, that advanced the capital-intensive growth in our society.

I was just reading an article that describes it quite well, that we now have an economy of "financialization," i.e., the taking of quick money profits instead of actually advancing our manufacturing, our industrial growth, and the development of our skilled labor. The article describes how financialization is starving manufacturing, because a lot of start-up companies are having a very hard time getting capital and the tax credits they need to get started, which hurts manufacturing, and it strangles new ideas in science and technology.

This is what we're up against right now, and this is why I have been in the forefront of fighting for the economic approach embodied in Lyndon LaRouche's Four Economic Laws, starting with the re-imposition of Glass-Steagall. We would already have this—and many other positive measures as well—if we didn't have people like Al Green in Congress.

The election is less than two months away. In Texas we have an early voting process, which begins October 22.

This is what we now see going into this election. This may be the most important national election in our lifetimes, not only for the people of the 9th Congressional District, but for every citizen in the nation.

## No Visible Support for Al 'Impeachment' Green

**EIR:** Before we conclude, could you say a little more about Al Green, just so it is as clear as possible?

**Rogers:** The key to this is, who is lining Al Green's pocket book? He is one of the richest Congress members, worth millions of dollars. He sits on the Financial Services Committee, and his District is one of the poorest, with one of the highest crime rates in the country. I think those facts really need to be contrasted with the breakdown that ordinary men, women, and their families are experiencing, and contrasted to my platform for economic growth to do away with, as I said before, the war policy, the regime change policy, the drug trafficking.

I will finish by saying this: One thing that's very important for people to know in this election, especially if they live in the 9th Congressional District and have the opportunity to vote for me: I'm running as an Independent. And to go back to the first question you asked, which is, do people see the Independent campaign as just a lost cause? Well, I'm the only Independent candidate, that is going toe to toe in standing up in defense of the President against the ongoing coup. My Independent candidacy and my platform represents a more important and greater potential than any campaign out there, a greater power and potential for actually addressing the future needs of our country right now, making sure we shut down the British Empire control over our American System and the institution of the Presidency.

I am running as an Independent, but in Texas, our election process still revolves around a two-party system of straight party votes for Republicans or else Democrats. We have to break that. I am calling on everyone to break their straight party ticket and deliberately and decisively vote for me. Look for my name on the ballot: Kesha Rogers, Independent for Congress. It's there.

That is an important message, because unless voters do that, they're going to miss the opportunity to vote for me. There's no Republican running in the District, so voters have to go and vote for me as an Independent.

We have been non-stop on the campaign trail. We have a sound truck going around the District. We are dropping in at local businesses and going to community events, where I've received a very positive response. There is almost no visible support for Al Green. There is a large, international community in the 9th CD, including Chinese, Vietnamese, Nigerian, and Caribbean,

algreen.house.gov

*Rich and angry, Democratic Party incumbent Rep. Al Green is the poster boy pushing for the impeachment of President Donald Trump.*

including Haitian. There is also a large Latino constituency in the District. My platform of bringing the United States on board the Belt and Road Initiative has resonated very strongly among these groups. This has also been the case for American-born constituents, among labor especially.

I have spoken before a number of these groups, and I have also addressed a number of political meetings of Republicans and other groups, on the importance of this election for the future of mankind. I have received an overwhelming response of support. I have a national team of phone-bank callers and others, organizing to get the word out on the national importance of this campaign for the future of all of us, and recruiting people in the District to support me.

**EIR:** Thanks so much.

# The Leaders of the United States, China, Russia, and India Must Take Action!

We, the undersigned, appeal to President Trump, President Putin, President Xi Jinping and Prime Minister Modi, to convoke an emergency summit in order to create a New Bretton Woods global monetary system.

To review the full petition and to add your own signature, visit: bit.ly/sign-nbw

## Elected Representatives

*(active or former federal, state, or local elected officials)*

Senator Richard Black (USA)
Sitting Virginia State Senator (Republican, District 13)

Hon. Gianni Tonelli (Italy)
Sitting member of the Italian Chamber of Deputies, Lega Nord party

Prof. Ivo Christov (Bulgaria)
Sitting Member of the Bulgarian parliament for the Socialist Party, member of the Foreign Policy, and Science and Education committees

U.S. Senator Mike Gravel (USA)
Two-term Democratic senator for the state of Alaska (1969-1981); famously read classified Pentagon Papers at a Congressional hearing to expose failure of the Vietnam War policy

Dr. Natalia Vitrenko (Ukraine)
Chair of the Progressive Socialist Party of Ukraine; member of parliament with the Socialist Party of Ukraine (1995-1998) and then with the Progressive Socialist Party of Ukraine (1998-2002)

Viktor Marchenko (Ukraine)
Former member of parliament, Progressive Socialist Party of Ukraine

Dr. Kirk Meighoo (Trinidad & Tobago)
Former Senator, Trinidad & Tobago; member of the advisory board of the Caribbean Integrationist

Senator William "Bill" Owens (USA)
Former Massachusetts State Senator (1975-1982, 1989-1992), Democratic Party

Souad Sbai (Italy)
Former member of Italian National Parliament

Commissioner Robert Van Hee (USA)
Sitting County Commissioner, District 4 Redwood County, Minnesota

Councilwoman Elena Fontana (Italy)
Former City Councilwoman, Italia-Montichiari (Brescia)

Mayor Henry Gonzalez (USA)
Former Mayor of South Gate, California, founder and former President of the Labor Council for Latin American Advancement

Cornelius Gallagher (USA)
U.S. Congressman, New Jersey (1959-1972), Democratic Party

## Government Officials

*(active or former military, diplomats, ambassadors, etc)*

General Edwin de la Fuente Jeria (Bolivia)
Former Commander-in-Chief, Bolivian Armed Forces

Dr. Julio C. Gonzalez (Argentina)
Former Technical Secretary to the Argentine Presidency

Major General (ret.) Kostas X. Konstantinidis (Greece)
Cofounder of the Non-Governmental Organization, "Amphiktyonia of Ecumenical Hellenism"

Alain Corvez (France)
Advisor on international strategy

James George Jatras (USA)
Former diplomat; former advisor to Republican Party Senate leadership

Jacques Bacamurwanko (Guinea)
Former Ambassador of Burundi to the USA; Now serving as Capacity Building Expert (Chef du Département "Suivi-Evaluation"), National Capacity Building Secretariat, in Guinea

Ambassador Leonidas Chrysanthopoulos (Greece)
Former ambassador; former Secretary General of the Organization of the Black Sea Economic Cooperation

## Organizational Leaders

*(leaders in labor, agriculture, industry, or business organizations)*

Daisuke Kotegawa (Japan)
Research Director, Canon Institute; Former Executive Director for Japan, IMF

Dr. Walter Formento (Argentina)
  Director, Center for Economic and Political Research
Jean-Pierre Gerard (France)
  Former member of the Council of Monetary Policies of the
  Banque de France; entrepreneur
John Lampl (USA)
  Vice-President (retired) of the AFL-CIO, North Dakota;
  former District President of North Dakota Democratic
  Party
Rich (John R) Anderson (USA)
  Former director of the National Cattlemen's Association;
  former member of the Texas Republican Executive
  Committee; former County Chairman of the Republican
  Party
George Bioletto (USA)
  Trustee, International Association of Machinists, Long
  Beach, California
Francis Kelly (USA)
  Farm Bureau in Wyoming; county chair in the Republican
  Party
Tate Ulsaker Nelson (New Zealand)
  International Trade Consultant; founder of Direct Info
Denys Pluvinage (France)
  President of Editions Apopsix publishing company

## Political, Religious, and Social Leaders

Helga Zepp-LaRouche (Germany)
  Founder and president of the Schiller Institute; founder and
  chairwoman of the German Bürgerrechtsbewegung
  Solidarität party (BüSo) (Civil Rights Movement Solidarity)
Fouad Al-Ghaffari (Yemen)
  Head of the Preparatory Committee of the New Silk Road
  Party in Yemen; President of the Yemeni BRICS Youth
  Cabinet
Reverend Andrew Ashdown (UK)
  Anglican Priest; author, *The Very Stones Cry Out*; leader of
  the first British community group to visit Aleppo following
  the beginning of the Syrian conflict
Ellen Brown (USA)
  Attorney; chairman of the Public Banking Institute; author
  of twelve books, including *Web of Debt* and *The Public Bank
  Solution*
Ali Rastbeen (France)
  President of the Geopolitical Academy of Paris
Chris Fogarty (USA)
  Former Vice President of the Friends of Irish Freedom;
  author of *The Mass Graves of Ireland: 1845-1850* and *Ireland
  1845-1850: the Perfect Holocaust, and Who Kept it Perfect*
Fred Huenefeld, Jr. (USA)
  Louisiana State Democratic Party Committee
Jacques Cheminade (France)
  President of Solidarité et Progrès
Tom Gillesberg (Denmark)
  Chairman of the Schiller Institute in Denmark
Ramasimong Phillip Tsokolibane (South Africa)
  Leader of LaRouche South Africa

Liliana Gorini (Italy)
  Chairwoman of the Movimento Internazionale per i Diritti
  Civili – Solidarietà (MoviSol)
Antonio "Butch" Valdes (Philippines)
  Founder of the Philippines LaRouche Society; Initiator of
  the Citizens National Guard, Philippines
Abdus Sattar Ghazali (USA)
  Editor, *American Muslim Perspective*; former News Editor
  of *Daily News*, Kuwait; former correspondent of Associated
  Press and the *Daily Dawn* of Pakistan
Michael P. Collins (USA)
  Author of *Saving American Manufacturing* and *The
  Manufacturer's Guide to Business Marketing*; writer for
  *Forbes* magazine and Industry Week
George/Vladislav Krasnow (USA/Russia)
  Russian American Goodwill Association
Mike Robinson (UK)
  Editor, UK Column, Plymouth, UK
Dr. James Hufferd (USA)
  911 Truth Grassroots Organization, Adel, Iowa
Mary Sullivan (USA)
  Irish American activist, Chicago, Illinois

## Leaders in the Arts and Sciences
*(scientists, technologists, professors, and musicians)*

Dr. Eduardo M.A. Peixoto (Brazil)
  PhD and Professor of Chemistry, University of São Paulo;
  former Superintendent of Technical Consultancy, National
  Development Bank (BNDES); former Brazilian representa-
  tive to World Health Organization
Dr. Jorge Alberto Montenegro (Argentina)
  Professor of International Trade, FASTA University
Professor Bong Wie (USA)
  Vance Coffman Endowed Chair Professor of Aerospace
  Engineering at Iowa State University; founding director of
  the Asteroid Deflection Research Collaboration
Gian Marco Sanna (UK)
  Founder of the Geminiani Project, focused on restoring the
  original classical music tuning of 432 Hz; leader of the
  Camerata Geminiani
Dr. Rainer Sandau (Germany)
  Technical Director, Satellites and Space Applications,
  International Academy of Astronautics (IAA)
Chief Scientist Wayne Moore, PhD (USA)
  Accel Algorithmics; NASA (ret.)
Tom Wysmuller (USA)
  NASA (ret.); meteorologist
Professor Lilya Takumbetova (Russia)
  Retired Associate Professor at Bashkir State Pedagogical
  University
Professor Cathy M. Helgason, MD (USA)
  Retired Professor of Neurology, University of Illinois
  College of Medicine, Chicago, Illinois
Roger Boyer (USA)
  Retired principal science and engineering technician at the
  Stanford Linear Accelerator (SLAC)

# A Crash is Looming, But a New Bretton Woods Is Within Reach!

by Brian Lantz and Harley Schlanger

Sept. 22—On July 25, 2007, as the first signs of the crisis began to emerge—the financial crisis that would ultimately lead to the collapse of Lehman Brothers and the near-collapse of the global financial system—economist Lyndon LaRouche opened a webcast with a warning that the system had reached a point of no return. He said:

> The world monetary financial system is actually now currently in the process of disintegrating. There's nothing mysterious about this; I've talked about it for some time, it's been in progress, it's not abating. What's listed as stock values and market values in the financial markets internationally is bunk! These are purely fictitious beliefs. There's no truth to it; the fakery is enormous. There is no possibility of a non-collapse of the present financial system—none. It's finished, now! The present financial system cannot continue to exist under any circumstances, under any Presidency, under any leadership.... Only a fundamental and sudden change in the world monetary financial system will prevent a general, immediate chain-reaction type of collapse.[1]

Unfortunately, the Bush and Obama administrations ignored LaRouche's warning—and his proposals—and the disintegrating "world monetary financial system" which LaRouche identified was not replaced. This has led to the crisis we face today.

Following the 2008 financial collapse, the systemic monetarist ideology at the core of the City of London and Wall Street system was carried forward. The decision to adopt a policy of "bailing out" the bankrupt system did not bring about a physical economic recovery, but secured a further rapid growth of cancerous debt and a continued "financialization" of the United States economy and the global economy as a whole.

During the last ten years, over $12 trillion in "quantitative easing" (QE) money has been issued under the bail-out policy, at the British Empire's direction and coordinated through the central banks of the United States, the European Union, Great Britain and Japan.

Rather than curing the patient, governments instead have fed the very disease which is killing the patient—scrambling to save the British monetarist empire by pumping money into the derivatives market, corporate stock buy-back strategies, mergers and acquisitions, and junk bonds—resulting in a situation in which the

---

1. Lyndon LaRouche webcast, July 25, 2007, published in *Executive Intelligence Review*, August 3, 2007.

financial parasites suck up all the new "blood" of virtually zero-interest rate liquidity, while investment in physical production evaporates.

This policy of "financialization" has further withered U.S. manufacturing, as recently reviewed in *Industry Week*, in an analytical piece titled, "How Financialization is Starving Manufacturing." The effects of using monetarist measurements of economic well-being are also seen in other ways. New business creation in the United States, for example, (i.e., the much-ballyhooed "start-ups") plunged to a total of only 414,000 businesses formed in 2015, the latest year surveyed, according to the U.S. Census data released in 2017. That compares to 500,000 to 600,000 new companies that were started in the United States *every year* from the late 1970s to the mid-2000s. As well, rural areas have been given a "death sentence."[2] The cost of all this, in human lives and misery, is almost beyond calculation, and will only be touched on here, briefly.

While industry and agriculture have been starved of credit, the reign of "quantitative easing" has actually done nothing to stabilize financial markets. The central banks of Europe, Japan and America are now themselves choking on a total of approximately $14.5 trillion equivalent (at face value) of bank, government and corporate financial paper that they have purchased since 2008.[3] This deployment of "helicopter money" has only increased financial indebtedness, while also producing a dramatic growth of the S&P 500 Index from its low in early 2009—this, itself, a sign of increasing financial instability, as "Ponzi scheme" financial betting replaces long-term productive investment.

**Debt as the Trigger**

An important feature of the building financial crisis has been the growth of corporate, government and personal debt. Worldwide, in the ten years since the 2008 global financial crisis, the debt held by nonfinancial corporations has grown by $29 trillion, and since 2007, the value of corporate bonds outstanding from nonfinancial companies has nearly tripled to $11.7 trillion, according to a McKinsey & Company piece, "Are We in a Corporate Debt Bubble?" The McKinsey article, written by Judy Lund, continues,

> Over the next five years, a record $1.5 trillion worth of nonfinancial corporate bonds will mature each year; as some companies struggle to repay, defaults will most likely rise.... The average quality of borrowers has declined. In the U.S., 22% of nonfinancial corporate debt outstanding comprises "junk" bonds from speculative-grade issuers, and another 40% are rated BBB, just one notch above junk. In other words, nearly two-thirds of bonds are from companies at a higher risk of default, including many U.S. retailers.

On September 20, former FDIC chair Sheila Bair also joined in warning of the danger of ballooning consumer and corporate debt.

The explosion of debt has reached such proportions that even normally "heads in the sand" media outlets, such as Bloomberg, Forbes and CNBC, have become increasingly and overtly frantic about a potential crisis. A slew of relevant articles in their publications appeared on or around September 15, the 10th anniversary of the collapse of Lehman Brothers Investment Bank.

With all of the talk of corporate and consumer debt, however, a far more deadly dimension of the crisis is now unfolding, a dimension rarely discussed, and one which you will not see addressed in the media outlets just mentioned. The hard reality is that unless the lurking issue of the quadrillion dollar market in speculative financial aggregates—most of it in the form of financial derivatives—is addressed, no attempt to get us safely out of the current crisis is possible. Since the crisis of 2008, this financial cauldron has been sustained at a roiling boil. This has been the consequence of "quantitative easing" as well as ever-softening "Too Big to Fail" bank reserve requirements and kindred measures.

The utter silence on the greatest danger that we face stems from the fact that those who run the central banks and other components of the financial system have refused to admit the actual nature of the 2007-2008 collapse. Many still insist on labeling that catastrophe as a "subprime mortgage" crisis, when even a cursory look at Lehman Brothers reveals that at the time of its collapse, it held approximately 930,000 over-the-counter (OTC) derivatives contracts.

---

2. See "Goodbye, George Baily: Decline of Rural Lending Crimps Small Town Business," *Wall Street Journal*, Dec. 25, 2017.
3. See "Central Bank Balance Sheets," Yardeni Research, Sept. 25, 2018.

## Derivatives: The Hydrogen Bomb

The actual, staggering dimensions of the looming financial collapse have, until recently, only been reported by the LaRouche movement, including Helga Zepp-LaRouche, Independent congressional candidates Kesha Rogers in Texas and Ron Wieczorek in South Dakota, the LaRouche Political Action Committee, and this publication.

Now, a small but significant number of independent analysts are beginning to speak up. For example, William White, former chief economist of the Bank for International Settlements, who along with Lyndon LaRouche was one of the few prescient voices speaking out before the 2008 Crash, told the German weekly *Der Spiegel* this week, that "the problems underlying the Lehman crisis have never been solved. On the contrary, they have turned worse." He added, "The debt is higher than ever before," criticizing the decision to print money to cover bad debt and arguing that the financial system is "crushing against a limit."

Additionally, the former chief economist of the IMF, Raghuram Rajan, who also forecast the 2008 crisis, is now warning of a domino effect which could be triggered by default, singling out the problem that the most risky sector of finance now resides in the "shadow banking system," in which there is no transparency. "Are there accidents waiting to happen? Yes, there are," he said in a recent interview.

The issue of corporate, government and personal debt, as large as these debts are, is only the lurking trigger on the estimated $1.2 quadrillion dollar financial derivatives bubble at the heart of the British Empire's *casino mondial.* A significant debt default, in so-called emerging markets or of corporate debt, would work like the nuclear fission trigger on a hydrogen (fusion) bomb. In the second quarter of 2018, insured U.S. banks had $207 *trillion* of exposure to derivatives, as known to the Office of the Comptroller of the Currency. In other words, the known exposure of these banks to derivatives contracts is *11 times the entire gross domestic product of the United States.*[4] Through "shadow banking" mechanisms the totals could be significantly higher.

---

4. Office of the Comptroller of the Currency, Quarterly Report on Bank Trading and Derivatives Activity, second quarter, 2018.

Institute for New Economic Thinking

*William White, former chief economist of the Bank for International Settlements.*

## Calls for a Return to Glass-Steagall

As the enormity of the current unfolding crisis begins to sink in with certain more astute members of the Establishment, it is not then surprising that there are again urgent calls from additional quarters, for a return to Glass-Steagall banking regulation with its implications.

Among the most prominent of the new calls for Glass-Steagall is a white paper issued by the U.S. credit union association, the National Association of Federally Insured Credit Unions (NAFCU). Its report, titled "Modernizing Financial Services: The Glass-Steagall Act Revisited," was followed by a September 11 op-ed in *The Hill* by the organization's Executive Vice President for Government Affairs and General Counsel, Carrie Hunt. While understating the danger of a financial crash today, the subtext of Hunt's piece is clear: By not restoring Glass-Steagall after the Crash of 2008, the speculative orgy of the "Too Big to Fail" banks that precipitated the crash when housing prices collapsed—which she characterizes as "excessive, unbridled risk taking"—absolutely continues today.

By not acting to ensure that, "banks' past misdeeds are not normalized or accepted as status quo," U.S. lawmakers' protection of the TBTF banks means that nothing was done to prevent the growth of these banks, and the size of their debt holdings has swelled to unsustainable levels, which Hunt says "will have a catastrophic impact on the American economy and wreak havoc on consumers' financial well-being." Hunt writes that a "modern approach" to Glass-Steagall—

would restrict the banks' ability to make risky

bets with consumers' savings and reduce their overall size, thereby limiting the likelihood of future bailouts and economic turmoil.

Similar warnings, and calls for Glass-Steagall measures, are also now being voiced in Europe. Among these is the former chairman of Sparda Bank, a Munich-based savings bank, Günter Grezga, who identified "deregulation" of banking as the cause of the 2008 financial crisis. He proposed a "Trennbanken system" (banking separation, as in Glass-Steagall), so that "the crisis not be repeated." His appeal was covered on September 11 on the Austrian website, kontrast.at.

The same theme was sounded in a column in the German *Finanzmarktwelt* on September 6, whose author, Claudio Kummerfeld, calls for a bank separation law modeled on Glass-Steagall. Reporting on the systemic threat posed by the unraveling of Deutsche Bank, he says that under a separation law, the bank could be broken up, which would allow a separate investment bank based in London to go under, without affecting "the deposits in a separated primary bank in Germany."

The political parties that now make up the new government of Italy have already called for Glass-Steagall

National Archives

*President Franklin Roosevelt signing the Banking Act of 1933 (the Glass-Steagall Act). At his immediate right and left are the two most prominent figures in the bill's development, Sen. Carter Glass of Virginia and Rep. Henry Steagall of Alabama, June, 16, 1933.*

bank separation measures.

The original 1933 Glass-Steagall legislation was an important element of Franklin Roosevelt's New Deal, which also emphatically required a national credit institution (the Reconstruction Finance Corporation was put to use) and national credit. The leading features of Glass-Steagall were the establishment of a wall of separation between commercial and investment banks, and an insurance program to protect depositors, implemented by the FDIC.

The repeal of Glass-Steagall in 1999 by the Gramm-Leach-Bliley Act, with the support of leaders of both U.S. political parties, opened the door for an orgy of speculative swindles, allowing commercial banks to buy and sell "instruments of financial innovation," such as "derivatives" and "swaps," which are in reality worthless pieces of paper, "bets" with no underlying value. With the repeal of Glass-Steagall, the U.S. government, including the FDIC, now stood behind all of these casino bets. The blowout of the Mortgage-Backed Securities bubble, which had been pumped up by speculative lending from deregulated financial institutions after Glass-Steagall was repealed, was the actual trigger for the Crash of 2008.

Indeed, days after the July 25, 2007 webcast cited in the opening of this article, Lyndon LaRouche drafted an emergency bill, the Homeowners and Bank Protection Act (HBPA), which specified what he meant by adopting "a fundamental and sudden change." Incorporating the basic principles of Glass-Steagall, LaRouche's proposal would have put the entire banking system through a Franklin Roosevelt-style bankruptcy reorganization. Taking such action would have frozen trillions of dollars of worthless assets, to be written down, or written off entirely, and there would have been no such category created as a

*Lyndon LaRouche delivering his "End of the Post-FDR Era" webcast, Washington, D.C., July 25, 2007.*



bank "Too Big to Fail," and no multi-trillion dollar bailout package to save them.

His draft bill would have protected the legitimate functions of banks, to allow them to disburse hundreds of billions of dollars of productive credit, issued by the U.S. government, which would have been channeled first into job creation in productive infrastructure, with an emphasis on the most modern technologies in high-speed rail construction, nuclear power production, and water and power management. This would have reversed the collapse of physical goods production and employment, which began with President Nixon's August 1971 decision to end Roosevelt's post-war recovery plan associated with the Bretton Woods system. A number of state and local governments passed resolutions in support of the HBPA, but the City of London and Wall Street stopped its introduction into the Congress.

## LaRouche's Full 'Four Laws' Required

In 2014, Lyndon LaRouche issued, "The Four New Laws to Save the U.S.A. Now! Not an Option; An Immediate Necessity" (https://larouchepac.com/four-laws).

In that document, LaRouche defines the only legitimate and scientifically accurate approach to econom-

ics, one which will secure future progress for the human species. Here, Man, not money or "supply and demand," are placed at the center of economics. Mr. LaRouche specifies that the U.S. government must now be charged with the responsibility, "to institute four specific, cardinal measures: measures which must be fully consistent with the specific intent of the original U.S. Federal Constitution." The Four New Laws feature reinstatement of Franklin Roosevelt's original Glass-Steagall banking separation act; a return to a national banking system; U.S. federal credits uttered to build a new U.S. infrastructure platform and a high technology, high-productivity economy; and a crash "science driver" program to develop fusion power and greatly expand NASA's human space exploration program.

LaRouche points out that the "four new laws" are a unity and must be grasped as a unity. This unity embraces humankind itself—the true identity of every human being as a potential genius—and provides the opportunity (physical, moral, and emotional) for every individual to lead a functionally productive, and by implication, immortal, life. The "four specific cardinal measures" taken as a unity are the means to achieving this rebirth, this *renaissance*, of our nation.

LaRouche's economic approach is based on *physical science,* i.e., Man's creative discoveries, which constantly redefine our relationship to the universe around us. This is LaRouche's *Science of Physical Economy,*[5] developed through his study of the discoveries of scientists and physical economists of the past, such as Johannes Kepler, Gottfried Leibniz and Bernhard Riemann. He made advances on their work through his own unique discoveries, parallel to the earlier "American" approach of Benjamin Franklin and Alexander Hamilton.

For LaRouche and these scientists mentioned above, an economy is not about financial profits or "monetary theory"—which has been the basis of all neo-liberal economic "theory," a thinly-disguised justification for looting populations, and one which has been hege-

5. See: *So, You Wish to Learn All About Economics*, by Lyndon La-Rouche.

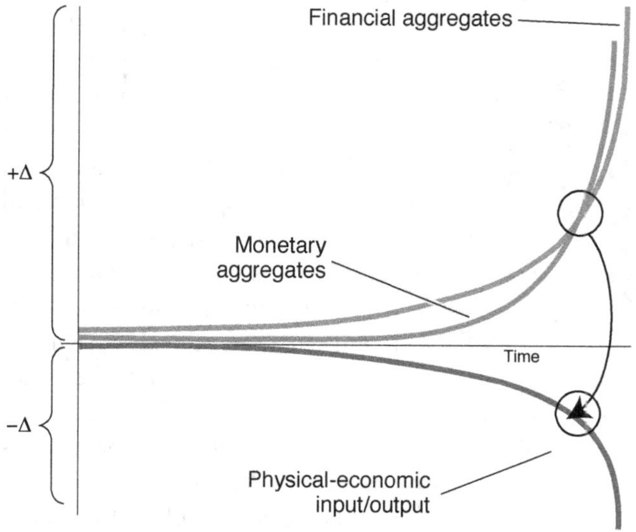

**The Collapse Reaches a Critical Point of Instability**



monic in the British Empire for 300 years. Rather, physical economics is about applying the most advanced scientific discoveries to the production and distribution of goods, to provide an improving standard of living for all people, while at the same time investing in the future, in areas which will lead to the scientific and technological progress needed to provide for the next generations.

On the other hand, the current, continued exponential growth of global debt and the growth of the utterly fantastic derivatives *casino mondial* of fictitious wealth can only continue through the issuance of new borrowing and increasing debt. As an inverted pyramid, it is only held up by increasingly weakening streams of revenue (debt service) bled from the remaining real economy. And this is what we have seen, particularly in the United States over the recent decades. This has been rigorously presented in Lyndon LaRouche's series of heuristic "Triple Curves" of a "typical collapse function,"[6] as the hyperbolic growth of financial and monetary aggregates, sustained by the third curve, the downward-plunging curve of the actual physical inputs/outputs of the real economy.

At the current moment, the growth of the global derivatives market appears to have fallen slightly, ostensibly due to "trade compression efforts." However, the

___

6. For LaRouche's Triple Curves, see Dennis Speed's presentation in the August 31, 2018 issue of *EIR*.

quadrillion dollar derivatives bubble remains as the main explosive, and the debt is the now-ticking detonation charge.

For example, in the "emerging market" economies, fueled by the speculative dollar carry-trade, these nations are saddled with more than $8 trillion in corporate and sovereign debt, of which more than $249 billion comes due in the next year. With rising interest rates, and a stronger dollar, speculators are fleeing from these emerging markets and their currencies, making dollar-denominated debt payments far more costly, and defaults inevitable. Witness the current currency and economic crises in Turkey and Argentina, systemically spilling over into Europe and Europe's banks—and then into the United States through derivatives "hedging."

Along with emerging market debt, U.S. corporate debt, student loan debt, and car loan debt have all grown exponentially, and all of this debt is then "securitized" into derivatives products, in the way that mortgage-backed securities are. The growing debt is the live "detonator."

This is the terminal condition of the process described by LaRouche's "collapse function," and President Donald Trump's actions, as valiant and well intentioned as they have been—as President he cannot succeed without our help. The demands to "save the cancer!" come from the British Empire, via the central banks, City of London and Wall Street, intent on saving their global monetary system, which is indeed the British Empire itself. Given the collapse of the real economies of the "West" caused by this blood-sucking, this system can now collapse at any time, with catastrophic consequences.

The reality of this crisis is now increasingly being acknowledged. The immediate threat to be addressed is the global debt bomb of derivatives, and the explosive charge of debt, built up by what have been unlimited flows of Central Bank quantitative easing and accompanying measures. The "bomb" could simply be detonated by the Federal Reserve attempting to now "taper" QE and raise interest rates.

The realization that one must take away from all of this, however, is that this crisis is fundamentally not about financial paper and algorithms. The matter at hand is existential for mankind as the failing British Empire's monetarist financial system has already riven the world. It is this failing and homicidal British Empire

EIRNS/Eli Santiago

*LaRouche PAC organizing for LaRouche's Four Laws in New York City, June 28, 2018.*

that is threatening a geopolitical "Thucydides Trap" and thermonuclear war, attempting to manipulate the United States against its natural allies Russia and China and their growing "South-South" alliance for cooperation and peaceful development.

## President Trump and Solutions Today

The Belt and Road Initiative of China's President Xi Jinping is already transforming much of the world, engendering optimism about the future. Even if censored and blocked out in the mass media, a multitude of projects and people-to-people exchanges have made enormous, positive changes in the relations among nations and made physical changes on the ground. As a consequence of the Trump presidency and the Belt and Road, and the influential ongoing work of the LaRouche movement, the "fundamental and sudden change" that economist and statesman Lyndon LaRouche called for in 2007 can be fully realized now!

This change is now the substance of the urgent call by Helga Zepp-LaRouche, founder of the Schiller Institutes, as well as the intervention of the national flagship campaign of Kesha Rogers, Independent candidate for Congress in the Texas 9th Congressional District. The urgent requirement now, as emphasized by those two leaders, is for the convening of a "Four Powers" summit of President Trump, President Xi Jinping, President Vladimir Putin and Prime Minister Modi. *The purpose of that summit is the prompt creation of a New Bretton Woods financial system, of fixed exchange rates and sovereign credit, replacing a now collapsing monetarist dis-order with a New Paradigm of "win-win" development.* The Donald Trump Presidency means that a New Bretton Woods summit among the leaders of the four leading—but very different—nations of the U.S., Russia, China and India, can now be organized.

This New Bretton Woods initiative is being taken to the United Nations this week, as well as to Capitol Hill in Washington, D.C., supported by prominent international endorsements. (See the Petition elsewhere in this issue.)

In July 2016, prior to the Republican convention, Trump shocked the bankers when he stated that he favored a return to Glass-Steagall bank separation. CNBC television reported that "Wall Street is not pleased" by this. Trump intervened directly in the Republican Platform hearings, insisting, along with campaign manager Paul Manafort, that Glass-Steagall be included in the party's platform. The plank said simply, "We support reinstating the Glass-Steagall Act of 1933, which prohibits commercial banks from engaging in high-risk investment."

Trump's commitment to Glass-Steagall was reaffirmed by spokesman Sean Spicer, following a meeting between Trump and community bankers in March 2017. The President answered a question from Bloomberg News on May 2, 2017, about whether he still supports Glass-Steagall, by saying, "I'm looking into that right now ... There's some people that want to go back to the old system [Glass-Steagall], right? So we're going to look at that."

Since his inauguration, President Trump has worked to revive U.S. manufacturing and, between the months of July 2017 and July 2018, the Bureau of Labor Statistics has reported a gain of 327,000 jobs in manufacturing, which is the largest gain since 1994-95. However, this increase in manufacturing job growth is not enough to turn the tide, given the ongoing collapse of U.S. in-

EIRNS/Sylvia Spaniolo

*LaRouche PAC organizing for LaRouche's Four Laws in New York City, June 9, 2018.*

frastructure, nor halt the huge "sucking sound" emitted from the City of London's "Square Mile" and from Wall Street.

The net physical economic output of the United States is negative. The real-world, physical consequences of disinvestment are just now being further highlighted by the devastating effects of Hurricane Florence in North and South Carolina, following the similarly disastrous hurricanes Harvey and Maria, the effects of which have not been mitigated. Nor has the prospect of future such threats been addressed. Likewise, consider the ongoing drought in the Western United States, with life-threatening water shortages and forest fires. It is also necessary to remind ourselves of the collapsing transportation grid in the New York City/New Jersey region, and consider the most recent "Report Card" of the American Society of Civil Engineers, which gave U.S. national infrastructure a grade of D+.

The continued destruction of the current and future creative and productive capabilities of the nation must be fully recognized and addressed. Causally, the continued collapse of physical economic activity is today visible in unemployment, destroyed living standards, the epidemic of heroin and other opioids, a skyrocketing suicide rate, and mass-killings that dominate our American landscape today.

This is an all-encompassing crisis, and agitation for

Glass-Steagall, by itself, is not sufficient. It only begins to address the underlying axioms, as presented by LaRouche. LaRouche's Four New Laws—and the approach to physical-economic development contained therein—are cardinal measures, and must further inform our drive for the leading four nations on the planet to convene a New Bretton Woods summit. It is the system of British monetarism itself which must be overturned, as Franklin Roosevelt acted against it in his time. American citizens are now weighing in, mobilizing with Texas Congressional candidate Kesha Rogers and the LaRouche PAC's national 2018 Campaign to Win the Future. This approach must become the affirmative policy of the U.S. government, and, as we demolish the Russiagate coup attempt, President Trump will be freed up to take these urgently required measures.

Lyndon LaRouche's university textbook on national economic policy, which also serves as a manual for government officials and advisors to governments.

# Eurasian Economic Forum Unites East Asia for Global Peace and Development

by Mike Billington

Sept. 23—This past month, two events in Asia have ushered in a new phase in the emergence of a new paradigm for mankind, uniting nations around the world in a common mission to end poverty and war—what Chinese President Xi Jinping calls "building a human community with shared destiny."

On Sept. 3-4, China hosted the summit of the Forum for China-Africa Cooperation (FOCAC), with every African nation represented (with one exception), in nearly every case by the head of state, in an enthusiastic demonstration of the optimism bursting forth across the formerly colonized nations, that ending poverty and achieving the status of modern industrial nations is finally a realistic dream, with China as the model demonstrating its feasibility.

Despite a growing chorus of attacks from the West describing the Belt and Road Initiative as a devious imperial plot to indebt nations and eventually take them over, the spirit of the New Silk Road is recognized across Africa, Ibero-America and Asia as the first opportunity for the so-called "developing nations" to finally and forever break free of neo-colonial backwardness through infrastructure and industrialization.

Then, on Sept. 11-12, Russian President Vladimir Putin sponsored the Fourth Eastern Economic Forum (EEF) in Vladivostok—an annual event since 2015—to bring together nations from around the world to participate in the development of the Russian Far East, which can be rightfully considered one of the last remaining "new frontiers" for mankind on Earth. The vast region, from Lake Baikal to the Pacific Ocean, comprises over 6 million square kilometers, but with a population of only about 6 million, leaving a population density of less than one person per square km. The population is

kremlin.ru

*Russian President Vladimir Putin addresses the 4th Annual Eastern Economic Forum, bringing together nations from around the world to participate in the development of Russia's Far East. Vladivostok, Russia, Sept. 11-12, 2018.*

concentrated in the southern areas, leaving most of the region totally unoccupied. Much of the land is mountainous or tundra, with difficult living conditions. Yet, through the use of technology, much of the territory can become productive in agriculture, mining and industry.

This year's EEF brought together over 6,000 participants from 60 countries, as well as more than 1,300 journalists. More than 220 investment agreements totaling

**Russian Far East**

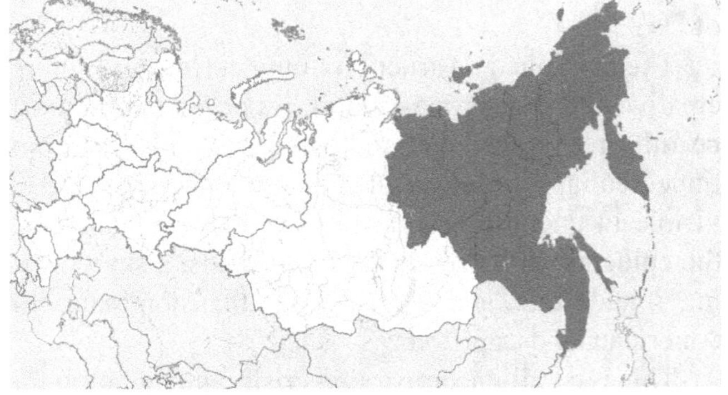

*Participants at the Eastern Economic Forum in Vladivostok, Russia, on Sept. 12, 2018.*



over $42 billion were signed. About half of the participants were Russian, with more than 1,000 from China, 570 from Japan, and 335 from South Korea. The six East Asian countries—Russia, China, Mongolia, Japan, and the two Koreas—were all represented. Presidents and prime ministers in attendance included Putin, Japanese Prime Minister Shinzo Abe, Mongolian President Khaltmaa Battulga, South Korean Prime Minister Lee Nakyeon, and President Xi Jinping, who was attending his first EEF. Both North and South Korea had high level delegations, but President Moon Jae-in and Chairman Kim Jong-un stayed behind, preparing for their third summit, which took place in Pyongyang on September 18-20, making dramatic progress towards denuclearization and peaceful development of the region.

Just as the FOCAC summit demonstrated the unity of the African nations in the spirit of the New Silk Road, so the EEF offered proof that all of Asia, and other nations as well, see the extension of the Belt and Road Initiative through North Korea and into the Russian Far East as a basis for hope for peaceful cooperation in a great undertaking for the benefit of all nations.

Those who follow only the mainstream media in the United States have no way of knowing that the world has changed, dramatically, as a result of these two international events. In the mindset of the Anglo-American oligarchy, that which does not fit into the zero-sum, geopolitical framework of western superiority simply does not exist.

## Connectivity Throughout Eurasia

Zhang Zongyan is the CEO of China Railway, which runs China's rail system across Asia, as well as New Silk Road lines from China to fifteen European cities, while actively building over a dozen rail lines in Africa. He reported to Xinhua on Sept. 17 that he had negotiated a plan during the EEF with the Russian Ministries of Transport and Development of the Far East, saying:

China Railway is looking at the Far East as one of the most important destination markets for extending its principal activity. Chinese enterprises are ready to deploy their own advanced technology, equipment, and engineering to take part in the construction of infrastructure in the Far East. This will contribute to the implementation of the Belt and Road Initiative and the development of cooperation between northeastern China and the Russian Far East.

This will include participation in the building of Primorye-1 and Primorye-2 transport corridors, connecting the Chinese provinces of Heilongjiang and Jilin with the Russian ports on the Pacific coast. (See *The New Silk Road Becomes the World Land-Bridge, Vol. 2*, pp. 95-105.)

Speaking at the EEF, North Korean Deputy Railways Minister Kim Yun Hyok announced a plan to reconnect North and South Korea by rail:

At the moment we are determined to connect the railways of North and South Korea. This is a fundamentally important project and it is necessary to provide the best possible conditions for this project to be finally implemented.

The plan is to have Russia, North Korea and South Korea jointly build the railroad on the Korean East Coast, reaching Rason Port in North Korea near the Russian border. Russia has already reconstructed the rail line from Vladivostok to Rason, and had been transporting Russian coal to Rason, then on to South Korea via Hyundai Merchant Marine ships to South Korea, where it was loaded onto South Korean KORAIL rail cars and shipped to South Korean POSCO steel plants. This consortium between Russia, North Korea, and the three mentioned South Korean companies was a model for "peace through development" on the Korean penin-

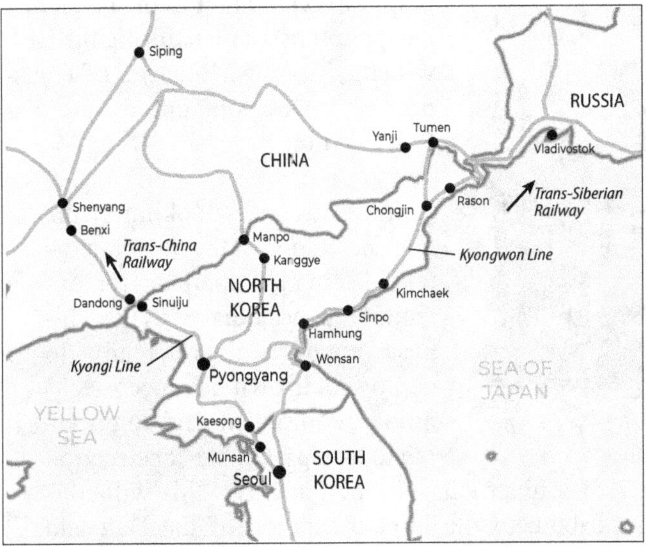


sula, until the previous South Korean government of President Park Geun-hye, under pressure from Obama to cut all relations with North Korea, did exactly that in February 2016.

It is only the active cooperation between Presidents Trump and current South Korean President Moon Jae-in, with full support from Russia and China, which has made possible an historic opening for peace and development in Korea, creating the current conditions for unity across all of Asia, as demonstrated at the EEF.

China is also fully engaged in the opening up of Korea's rail infrastructure. China's Liaoning Province, which borders North Korea, issued a plan coming out of the EEF for China to reconstruct the west coast rail line in North Korea, connecting Seoul with Pyongyang, then continuing on to Sinuiju on the Chinese border, and across the Yalu River on the Sino-Korean Friendship Bridge to Dandong in Liaoning Province. Plans for a new bridge, and a North Korea-China economic zone on Hwanggumpyong Island in the Yalu River between China and North Korea, are also in the plan.

Liaoning is setting up a group that "shares a common destiny in Northeast Asia by converging economic corridors that connect China, Russia, and Mongolia with a framework called the China-Japan-South Korea + X Model," linking all six East Asian nations via development corridors.

President Trump, in the video he presented to Chairman Kim Jong-un during their historic summit in Singapore on June 12, included visions of U.S., Chinese and Russian investments in North Korea, bringing the

"Hermit Kingdom," as it was known, into the emerging Asian economic dynamo. U.S. involvement in this effort is crucial, but Trump's freedom of action has been severely restricted by the ongoing British-instigated "Russiagate" coup attempt against him. The entire network of British and Obama Administration operatives running the coup attempt are now themselves being exposed for their crimes—which can, and must, free Trump to restore his commitment to friendly relations with Putin and Xi Jinping, and bring the United States into the New Silk Road development process internationally.

Asked about North Korea during the Q&A session of the EEF plenum, President Putin said: "Indeed, President Trump has shown an innovative approach to dealing with North Korea. I agree, this actually shows a certain amount of courage, political courage, and an innovative approach." He suggested that North Korea's need for security guarantees in order to give up its nuclear weapons was not only a U.S. concern:

> We have the format of the six-party talks. The international community can give such guarantees, including those secured by the presence of nuclear powers in these agreements. China and Russia are parties to these talks.... If North Korea is satisfied with U.S. guarantees alone, that is fine with us, but it is probably unlikely to happen. International guarantees would be more relevant in this case.

There could be no clearer example of the reality that Trump's commitment to friendly relations with Russia and China is on behalf of the crucial combination needed to bring peace and development to the world, and that those who are trying to bring him down are intent on war to preserve the dying British Empire.

**Russia-China-Japan**

There are two critical relationships in the new Asian dynamic: that between Putin and Xi, and that between Japanese Prime Minister Abe with both Russia and China. Putin and Xi held their third bilateral summit this year on the sidelines of the EEF, where they asserted that "regardless of the changes in the international situation, China and Russia will unswervingly promote their ties and steadfastly safeguard world peace and stability," as reported by the Chinese Ministry of Foreign Affairs. They pledged to further solidify the ties between the Belt and Road Initiative (BRI) and Russia's Eurasian Economic Union (EAEU), in the fields of energy, agriculture, scientific and technological innovation, and finance, including conducting their growing trade in local currencies rather that the U.S. dollar.

They also agreed to further expand "local cooperation" agreements, including between China's Northeast and Russia's Far East (as in the Liaoning rail plan discussed above), and between the Yangtze River basin and the Volga River basin.

Both leaders addressed the tense global strategic situation. Putin said, "Our relations are critical not only for our countries, but for the world as well." Xi remarked that the China-Russia partnership "allows us to jointly neutralize the external risks and challenges, and to assist in joint development."

*Russian President Vladimir Putin (left) meeting with Japanese Prime Minister Shinzo Abe, Nagato, Japan, Dec. 15, 2016.*

Putin accepted Xi's invitation to attend the second Belt and Road Forum in China, planned for 2019. In his speech to the EEF, Putin described the BRI as "a civilization-wide project for the future of mankind."

The importance of the role being played by Prime Minister Abe in this emerging new paradigm can not be over stated. While Japan remains America's closest ally in Asia, and despite the anti-Russia and anti-China hysteria in the West, Abe has unhesitatingly defended his intention to restore close relations with Putin, to finally achieve a peace treaty between the two nations—unresolved since WWII—and to have Japanese industry play a leading role in the development of the Russian Far East. Putin and Abe are intent on reaching an agreement over the sovereignty of the islands contested by the two countries, and then sign a peace treaty, all in the near term.

Japan's relations with China have also taken a dramatic turn for the better, with Abe now openly committed to joint development projects of the two industrial superpowers in third countries along the New Silk Road. Chinese Premier Li Keqiang visited Japan in May—the first high-level visit in eight years—where he announced Japan's intention to join the Belt and Road Initiative. In Vladivostok, Abe and Xi met the press after a private summit. Xi praised Japan's role in helping China's reform and opening up process since the signing of the China-Japan Treaty of Peace and Friendship exactly 40 years ago, noting: "The Belt and Road Initiative has provided a new platform and ex-

perimental field for China and Japan to deepen their mutually beneficial cooperation."

The first practical example of this cooperation emerged immediately after the EEF, when Thailand's Transport Minister Arkhom Termpittayapaisith announced on September 19 that Japan and China plan to jointly invest in Thailand's infrastructure projects, specifically a 176 kilometer high-speed rail connection from Bangkok to U-Tapao International Airport (the former U.S. B-52 airbase during the war on Indochina) on the eastern shore. This high-speed rail line will connect the capital with the rapidly developing industrial sites of the Eastern Seaboard Development Program, which has received significant Japanese support over the past decades.

Lyndon LaRouche and *EIR* have long proposed that the construction of the Kra Canal in southern Thailand would be the perfect project to bring China and Japan together for cooperation in development, given the huge benefit which the canal would bring to both countries, while solidifying peaceful relations between them. The joint, high-speed rail project should advance the needed cooperation, which could then move on to the Kra Canal in the near term.

### Transforming Vladivostok

President Putin is implementing a major transformation plan for Vladivostok, the hub of the international development of the Russian Far East. Japanese business leaders attending the EEF emphasized the huge potential for large-scale development invest-

The cable-stayed Russky Bridge in Vladivostok, Russia, completed in July 2012.

Airport was renovated and new tourist and business facilities were constructed both in Vladivostok proper and on Russky Island.

This year Putin took the next step. In his greeting to the EEF, he said:

> We are meeting here on Russky Island at the Far Eastern Federal University, where we intend to start a world-class education and research center, and develop it further. This includes, of course, construction of a technology park and a mega-science research installation that will allow solving completely new fundamental science and applied science tasks in pharmaceuticals, materials science and other spheres.

He called on Russia's leading companies to "build their engineering facilities, research and development centers on Russky Island. The Government and the top management of these corporations should consider this as direct instructions." He declared that the Far East will no longer be a backwater, but will be the "driving force of the national economy, innovations and culture."

Already, since 2016, Vladivostok has been the site of one of the world's greatest classical music festivals, the International Mariinsky Far East Festival, at the Mariinsky Primorsky Theater, organized by the world-famous director of the Mariinsky Theater in St. Petersburg, Valery Gergiev. The 2016 Festival was held in tandem with the EEF, with 27 operas and concerts over 12 days, with 300 international musicians and singers from 12 countries, and with over 20,000 visitors from around the world.

ments in the Far East, but noted that there are still significant problems to be resolved, such as poor infrastructure, high electricity costs, and the difficulty in securing human resources in the sparsely populated region.

Putin is addressing these problems. As he did with Sochi, where he was widely criticized for spending $50 billion to prepare the region for the 2014 Olympics, Putin has allotted huge sums over the past six years for the development of Vladivostok. His intent in Sochi was to create a modern, year-round resort which would more than pay for the investment. Indeed, six and a half million people visited Sochi in 2017.

A similar process in Vladivostok began when Russia hosted the 24th APEC Summit in 2012 in this Far Eastern city. Two new bridges were constructed— one over Zolotoy Rog Bay in the middle of the city, and one to Russky Island, where the Summit was held. At 1,104 meters, the Russky Bridge is the longest cable-stayed bridge in the world. Vladivostok International

Poster for the 3rd International Far East Festival, 2016.

This captures the vision of the new paradigm— launching a scientific and cultural renaissance embracing all of mankind, while taking on the development of even the most desolate areas of the world, such as the Russian Far East and the Arctic, and, eventually, the Moon and Mars.

# What a Miserable Spectacle! Germany Needs Another Policy!

by Helga Zepp-LaRouche, Chair of the German political party *BüSo*, the Civil Rights Movement Solidarity

Sept. 22—If one understands "theater of the absurd" to mean the representation of disoriented people in a meaningless world, then we are now witnessing a gala performance of the genre in Berlin. What is demonstrated by the scandal around the former head of the *Bundesamt für Verfassungsschutz* [Germany's FBI], Hans-Georg Maassen, who was kicked upstairs as a result of his blindness on the right; the irresponsible behavior of Interior Minister Horst Seehofer; and the personal efforts of Chancellor Merkel and SPD chair Andrea Nahles to remain in power—is that the Berlin establishment is in the wrong film. They are acting out the script of a world which only exists in their heads, and has nothing to do with the reality of the normal population or with strategic developments. If Germany is to avoid severe damage, we urgently need a new policy!

If Seehofer calls migration the "mother of all problems," then he himself and the geopolitical neo-liberal paradigm that he represents are the "grandmother of all problems." Because there would be no refugee crisis in this form, if Bush, Obama, Blair, and Cameron had not waged wars in Southwest Asia on the basis of lies, violations of international law that are never addressed by the German establishment. A glaring proof of their complicity is the announcement by Economy Minister Altmeier of the sale of new weapons systems to Saudi Arabia, a country which is even now waging a war of annihilation against Yemen. If the world is to endure, this will have repercussions under international law!

And there would be no crisis in this form either, had Europe distanced itself from the policy of the colonial powers and the subsequent conditionalities of the IMF toward Africa. Had Europe pursued, over the past decades, the policy of industrialization of Africa that China has undertaken for around ten years, then the African refugees would have had no reason to leave their homes.

In light of these realities, the theater in Berlin is not only absurd, but also abominable. Maassen plays the

Bundesministerium des Innern/
Sandy Thieme
*Hans-Georg Maaßen*

CC/Sandro Halank
*Andrea Nahles*

*Horst Seehofer*

role of the fox in the henhouse, Seehofer the elephant in the china shop who knows no tomorrow, and Merkel the incredible shrinking Queen, while Nahles is cast as the nightmare of [former SPD leaders] Kurt Schumacher and Willy Brandt, who are turning in their graves. What a play! And then Nahles comes back as the inventor of a new Olympic sport: rowing backwards!

It is symptomatic that a proven cynic like *Spiegel* columnist Jan Fleischhauer puts his finger on the sore spot: Under the heading, "Feminist Porn Instead of the

Proletariat," he wrote Sept. 20 that the SPD leadership has long since lost sight of its voters. The SPD in Berlin and the Jusos (the SPD youth group) demand that such porn be "easily obtainable, permanent and free of charge," and therefore should be included in the media libraries of the national broadcasting companies ARD and ZDF. They are just crazy! It should be obvious to anyone that the whole left-liberal-green range of SPD issues, which completely ignores the existential concerns of former SPD voters—such as rents, poverty in old age, health inequities, and lack of future prospects—is the reason that the SPD has lost ten million voters since 1998.

*Press conference with Prime Minister of Hungary Viktor Orban and Russia's President Vladimir Putin following the Russian-Hungarian talks, Sept. 18, 2018.*

## Mogherini in Outer Space

The real problem is that the behavior of Seehofer, Merkel, Nahles and Co. increases the political disenchantment in this country by several orders of magnitude. The events of Chemnitz and other attacks unmistakably throw the shadows of the Weimar Republic on the wall. Unfortunately, it can not be denied that only 73 years after the end of the Second World War, fascism can once again become a danger. After the "West" had supported the Nazi coup in Kiev in February 2014—in which Germany had its own axe to grind, but was rewarded with "F ... k the EU!" by Victoria Nuland—President Putin warned this would give a boost to fascist movements throughout Europe. Unfortunately, that is just what is developing before our eyes now.

Major responsibility for the current crisis must be attributed to the mainstream media, which have long since stopped revealing the truth as Seymour Hersh did in the case of the My Lai massacre, or Robert Parry in the case of lies about the alleged use of chemical weapons by President Assad. Instead, these media have long provided the "narrative" for regime change of inconvenient governments, glorified payments to terrorist organizations as "humanitarian aid," or orchestrated an enemy image of Russia or China through consistent negative coverage, depending on whatever fits the geopolitical strategy of the "Western" camp.

Meanwhile, the EU is busy accelerating the centrifugal forces in Europe; the most recent examples are Brussels' attacks on Poland and Hungary—which in the latter case have encouraged Hungarian Prime Minister Orban to pay a much more pleasant visit to Moscow. And exactly five years after the launching of China's Silk Road Initiative—which in the meantime has grown to include the greater part of humanity in the dynamics of a new paradigm of win-win cooperation—the EU comes out with its counter-proposal to the New Silk Road—the "European style"of improving connectivity with Asia on the basis of clear "rules." EU foreign policy chief Mogherini claims that she traveled to 20 countries in Eurasia, all of which expressed greater interest in the European proposal for improving connectivity, than in cooperation with the Chinese Silk Road. It would be interesting to know what planet these 20 states are located on, because the vast majority of Eurasian countries have long been working together with China and Russia for their own benefit.

But China responded to the EU initiative in its usual cooperative way, and welcomed it: we should join hands and cooperate in the development of Eurasian infrastructure, they proposed, and the EU and China should act as partners rather than rivals.

What applies to Eurasia pertains obviously even more to the perspective of Europe-China cooperation with respect to the development of Africa. For example, Professor Nader Habibi of Brandeis University wrote Sept 20 in *China Daily,* that despite Europe's claim to be Africa's main trading and investment partner, Africa does not appear to have developed economically as a result of this relationship. China's commitment, by contrast, opens up the potential to create millions of jobs. Therefore, China's economic activities in Africa are absolutely in the interest of Europe, if it seeks a real solution to the refugee crisis, wrote Habibi.

## A Great Vision for Humanity's Future

The new Italian government is already fully on this path. Finance Minister Giovanni Tria and the Undersecretary of State in the Italian Ministry of Development, Michele Geraci, have just signed a memorandum of understanding with China to work together on the industrialization of Africa to overcome the refugee crisis.

Minister of Economic Development and Deputy Prime Minister Luigi Di Maio expressed his satisfaction that Italy is the only European country to hold far-reaching negotiations with China on the New Silk Road, which could probably be concluded by the end of the year. Di Maio says:

China-Italy Chamber of Commerce

*Prof. Michele Geraci, Undersecretary of the Italian Ministry of the Economic Development, introduces the Task Force China in Shanghai, August 31, 2018.*

> The man who introduced China to Europe was an Italian, and an extraordinary one: Marco Polo…. Like Marco Polo, I will be fully committed to the New Silk Road because, as deputy Chinese Prime Minister Hu [Chunhua] said yesterday, the arrival point of the Silk Road is Rome, and Italy can not help but be a fundamental partner of China's economic belt initiative.

That should be an inspiration to us in this country. What we need in Germany is a new combination of forces that will put a new policy for cooperation with China and Russia on the agenda for solving the key strategic challenges, notwithstanding the rearguard actions of the not-so-large Grand Coalition. Instead of continued rejection by North African countries that refuse to set up concentration camps for African refugees in their countries, and instead of completely ruining the image of the EU (which is already very tattered) through the military use of Frontex (the EU's border and coast guard agency) in the Mediterranean against refugees in boats, we should instead respond immediately to Xi Jinping's offer to industrialize the African continent together with China.

What is completely lacking in German politics so far, is a great vision for the future of humanity, and that is exactly what China has been placing on the agenda for five years. The spirit of the New Silk Road has long captured the imagination of the majority of countries in the world: the idea of an unprecedented division of labor in the common interest, to shape a future that will not only overcome poverty throughout the planet in a short time, but can also realize the potential of all humans on this earth.

What is needed now are people in our country who are able to rise far above the pussyfooting of the above-mentioned actors, people who practice the art of self-reflection instead of "groupthink," and who do not leave the fate of Germany to groupings which have already had their chance, but failed to use it.

There is every reason to be optimistic—but we need to act. We have the concept: "The New Silk Road becomes the world land-bridge!"

*zepp-larouche@eir.de*

November 10, 2009

WHAT YOUR ACCOUNTANT DOESN'T KNOW

# The Science of Society

by Lyndon H. LaRouche, Jr.

*The fact is, that for more than half-a-century, all accountants and most economists have been repeatedly wrong, whereas, during the same half-century all of the forecasts which I have actually presented have been "on the mark." There are two reasons for my unique success during that period. It is not that I am a better accountant than they were; the difference is that I practice economics as a science. I am not alone. For example: lately, a growing number of academic and related kinds of leading specialists in the subject of national economy, have shown deep insight into the reasons for my unique success. Get to know this subject as we do. Your life might depend upon it: very soon.*

*In the meantime, the world economy, or, a very large part of it, including, especially western and central Europe and the Americas, is now at the brink of yet another of the steps downward toward the doom which awaits nations which refuse to make those necessary changes in policy-shaping which I emphasize here.*

### On the Subject of My Background in Economics:

As I have reported in numerous published locations, my record of superior competence in economy was rooted in my adolescent rejection of that folly named Euclidean geometry, in favor of a concept of economy as a branch of Leibniz's argument in physical science.[1]

My progress beyond my adolescent, anti-Euclidean, fascination with Leibniz, was continued during the immediate post-war years, in my role as, briefly, an admirer, but, then, by 1957-59, an opponent of the radical positivist methods of Professor Norbert Wiener and John von Neumann, an opposition which led to my conversion to the standpoint of Bernhard Riemann's 1854 habilitation dissertation by 1953. All my economic forecasts, beginning with a near-term forecast of the February-March outbreak of the relatively deep 1957-1959 recession, have been premised on the case for a physical science of economy based on the principles of Riemann.

The generally publicized features of my work as a forecaster, began to be more widely known through a restatement of a long-range forecast which I had first uttered during the 1959-1961 interval. I forecast that, unless certain changes in direction of U.S. policy-shaping were made by no later than the mid-1960s, we must expect a deep U.S. recession, or worse, to emerge during the last half of the decade. The assassination of President John F. Kennedy, assured the

---

1. Although the discovery of the concepts which Euclid parodied, had been made by competent authorities working in the tradition of Sphaerics earlier, the a-priori scheme of Euclid himself was a fraud. Competent geometry is the geometry of physical curvature, such as the adoption of the catenary by Filippo Brunelleschi, and Gottfried Leibniz's related universal principle of physical least action.

worst choice which would be made by his successors. That 1959-61 forecast of mine, as I have reaffirmed it during the later 1960s, hit with a succession of downward developments in the U.S. physical economy during the 1968-1973 interval, including the Nixon Administration's launching of the break-up of the tattered remains of the Bretton Woods System in August 1968.

I had been the only known economist to have foreseen such a pattern of ensuing developments embedded within the 1968 and following events. The uniqueness of my success as a forecaster, among then notable economists, led both to my celebrity, in a December 2, 1971 Queens College debate with a leading British Keynesian, Abba Lerner, and to the ever-lasting hatred thrown against me, internationally, up to the present moment, by associates of that European Congress for Cultural Freedom associated with such as Abba Lerner's colleagues of the intellectually and morally depraved Congress for Cultural Freedom, such as my virtually life-long, and unscrupulous adversaries Professor Sidney Hook and John Train.

Since that time, there have been three kinds of essential differences between my role in the profession, and those of what might be fairly named as the opposing "Brand X" varieties of academic alternatives.

**First:** I adhere to a concept of physical economy which has been characteristic of the constitutional American System of political economy, since the pre-1688 Massachusetts Bay Colony of the Winthrops and Mathers, the so-called Hamiltonian system on which our Federal Constitution was founded.

At the same time, I have been often an ally of some with whom I differed respecting the principles of economy, but with whom a certain practical degree of common cause was to be sought, such as certain Marxists with whom I agreed on certain issues, but never as a matter of an actual scientific method. My differences with those with whom I have sometimes

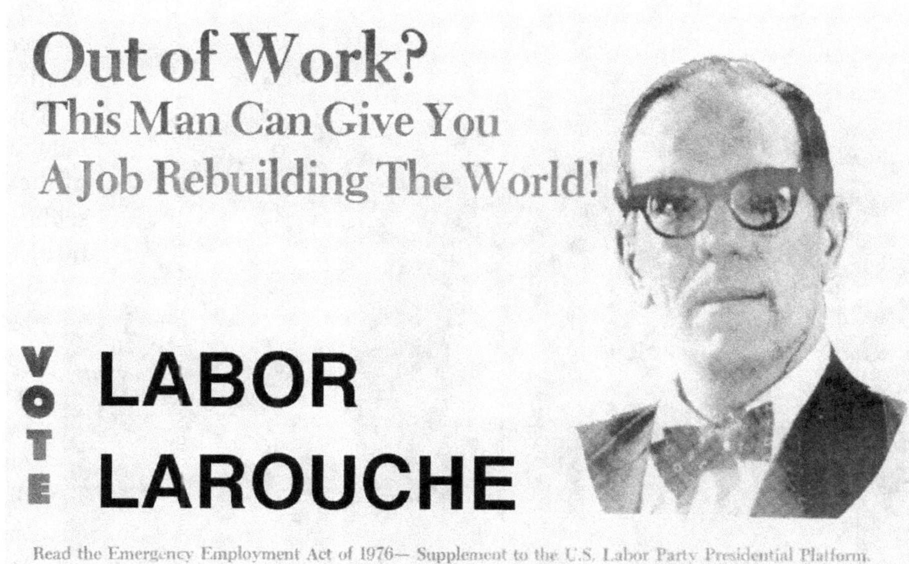



EIRNS

*A poster from Lyndon LaRouche's first campaign for the Presidency, in 1976. Throughout his life as an economist, he has had three essential and consistent differences with the "Brand X" academic alternatives.*

cooperated as a matter of an issue of common cause, have always been of that character.

**Second:** I have always insisted that real economy has the essential characteristics of a physical economy, rather than a monetary system. A system of money is a needed convenience for dealing with matters in the relatively small, but the success or failure of a national system is what it does, or fails to do as a physical-economic system. The inevitably terrible effects of monetary systems can be avoided only by means including the imposition of a fixed-exchange-rate principle among national systems.

**Third:** I have always insisted that the source of net physical profit, per capita and per square kilometer, of any economy, depends upon the characteristically anti-entropic, mustering and application of discovery and application of fundamental physical principles.

A sound form of modern nation-state economy, is one in which the closely related systems of currency and credit are maintained in more or less fixed terms of relevance, but in which both the productive power of labor and physical capital-intensity are increased through the intended effects of physical-scientific and Classical-cultural progress.

Presently, some leading economists of the world have come to understand the basis for, and implications

*Alexander Hamilton, the first U.S. Treasury Secretary, established the National Bank in Philadelphia, shown here. "Such a bank," he wrote, "is not a mere matter of private property, but a political machine of the greatest importance to the State."*



of the method expressed by my now widely known "Triple Curve" of interplay of financial, monetary, and physical changes. From consideration of the implications of that "Triple Function," the needed alternative, a double function, in terms of financial and physical "curves," is the remedy for the risk inherent in tolerating a monetarism-dominated system based on the three functions of monetary, financial, and physical organization of a national or world economy.

## The American System

As I have emphasized in various published, or otherwise more or less widely publicized locations, except for the special case of the U.S. Federal constitutional system of Franklin, Washington, Alexander Hamilton, et al., other cases, such as the generally well-known phases of combined west-Asian and European social-economic systems known since Sumer and Babylon, have been dominated by forms of supranational domination, properly defined as imperialisms, which are also characterized as pro-imperialist *monetarist* systems, such as that prescribed by John Maynard Keynes and his admirers.

By contrast, the American System, as launched by the New England succession of the Plymouth settlement and the Massachusetts Bay colony led by the Winthrops, and Mathers, was not created by persons enrolled in the function of refugees, but, rather of those implicitly acting in the footsteps of Cardinal Nicholas of Cusa, to bring the best fruits of European cultures to a new continent, where they could flourish free of the monetarist evils then represented, as still today, by the Venetian monetarist tradition. The essential distinction between the American System, so defined, as by the foundations of this republic, is that of a credit system, as opposed to the intrinsically imperialist mode of that monetary system which has remained the dominant feature of the subject economies of Europe since Babylon, Cyrus, the cult of Delphi, and Venetian imperial domination of Europe's national economies by monetarist systems, to the present day.

The pathological element which binds together victims such as the G-8 or G-20 as slaves of a London-centered, international monetarist tyranny today, is the prevalent, mistaken belief that money as such is a standard measure of economic value. That is a delusion taught by such as accounting professionals as a tenet of their practice still today. That is the delusion which has paved the pathway of folly carrying mankind as a whole to an immediately threatened destiny of global doom.

Viewing the great crisis now controlling the entire planet from that indispensable standpoint: the standpoint of the American System of political-economy, the standpoint which must now replace all of the financial-monetary systems of western and central Europe, and of central and South America now: if those regions are to survive the crisis-ridden weeks and months immediately ahead.

# I. The LaRouche System

Call what is the urgently needed alternative "The LaRouche System," with the understanding that this means the same thing, in principle, as the system of credit ("scrip") employed with great, if relatively brief success by the Massachusetts Bay Colony, prior to the colony's disruption by, first, James II, and, more significantly, the evil William of Orange.

Think of what I propose here and now, as being the same thing as the credit system specified by Benjamin Franklin's proposal for a "paper currency," and Alexander Hamilton's notion of a credit system. The goal is that of establishing a global system of fixed-exchange-rates among a set of what are respectively sovereign, fervently anti-monetarist, national credit systems. Under a two-function system (a financial credit system and a physical system), the value of money then becomes whatever the fixed-exchange-rate credit-system defines value to be.

To be emphatic, the source of the definition of value is not some calculated value attributed to the products of a sovereign nation; the value lies essentially, in the last analysis, entirely within the functioning of a fixed-exchange-rate credit-system, not the financial system as such. The function of the fixed-exchange-rate system is to provide a system of utterance of credit as the uttered debt of national republics, credit which is employed to support the increase, chiefly, of the fruitfulness of the productive powers of labor in each and all respective, sovereign republics. This may be credit extended for physical production, especially as advances in technology, but also for expansion of the scale of per-capita development of the physical-cultural potential of national economies.

The notion of economic value, so defined by a fixed-exchange-rate credit-system, is located in the relative improvement of the physical productive powers of labor, per capita and per square kilometer. The most appropriate way of defining that, pedagogically, today, is to think of these subject-matters in the Riemannian

U.S. Department of the Treasury

*Benjamin Franklin was an advocate of a paper currency, but he was no monetarist. "When the people find that they can vote themselves money," he quipped, "that will herald the end of the republic." And, "He that is of the opinion money will do everything may well be suspected of doing everything for money."*

terms of both Albert Einstein and Academician V.I. Vernadsky, but with special emphasis on Vernadsky's specifications of the respective roles of the Lithosphere, Biosphere, and Noösphere.

In general, that means that the "energy-flux density," and also the "physical investment" of the economy, per capita and per square kilometer is being increased. This means the increase of the physical basic economic infrastructure of the economy, is being increased per capita and per square kilometer, and that the productive powers of labor are being increased, per capita and per square kilometer of the economy as a whole.

These increases are effected through the fostering of the increase of the creative productive powers of labor of the entire economy, as this effect might be measured, in effect, in qualitative increase of the energy-flux density of both the relevant investment employed to increase the throughput of the productive process of the society as a whole, per capita and per square kilometer.

All measurements of value are to be subsumed by the aforesaid preconditions. This can be summarized by the statement, that a continuing increase of the energy-flux-density of human productive activity, per capita and per square kilometer, is the underlying, true measurement of the productive powers of labor, a measurement of relative productivity gained through what is essentially advances in Classical forms of artistic and scientific culture through fostering of the increase of the creative powers of the individual human mind.

*The Palabora copper mine in South Africa is the largest man-made hole in Africa: 2,000 meters in diameter and 762 meters deep. The looting of Africa has been an Anglo-Dutch imperial pastime for centuries, and remains so today.*

## Mining, or Looting?

Mining, as conducted by Anglo-American "capitalism" in Africa, for example, is not really productive in principle. Mining is productive only when it increases the wealth of the area in which mining is occurring; otherwise, mining is a process of depletion (e.g. "looting") as in Africa under predominantly British operations up to the present time.

Mankind must increase the productive powers of labor, through increase in capital-intensity of net investment in primary resources and productivity, per capita, and per square kilometer. If not, then the behavior of that relevant society is directed toward a relative lowering of the productive powers of labor and of natural resources. Thus, for example, "globalization" has represented an imminently genocidal destruction of the potential relative population-density of the planet, through destruction of developed regions, to effect production in less developed regions, while simultaneously destroying that in previously developed regions.

Take the case of China.

The development of China's economy as a cheap-labor source of production to replace that which had been occurring in Europe and North America, was based on a cheaper cost of labor, per capita, both in production, and in the population, per unit of output by China. This was, thus, essentially a new, globalized version of looting under the old Anglo-Dutch imperialist system. In effect, the per-capita income of the world was reduced to the lowered level we experience in, for example, both the U.S.A. since 1966-1968, and, more recently, in a partially industrialized China today.

The remedy must be to increase the investment in capital-intensity and basic economic infrastructure in the United States and China simultaneously, through relatively long-term, increasingly capital-intensive, productive capital-formation, that in both of these nations, simultaneously, through capital-intensive, high energy-flux-density modes of increase of the productive powers of labor, per capita and per square kilometer of area.

Thus, it must be said, value is not located within the domain of financial exchange as such. It is expressed, in one degree, within the bounds of the turnover of production and trade; but, the desired effect is a function of a notion of technology which is essentially increasingly capital-intensive, scientific-discovery-driven development of the economic process as a whole.

For example. Production in and of itself has an entropic effect, as the relatively richest and most accessible resources are depleted, and less rich, or less accessible resources must be employed, instead. Therefore, the net rate of increase of productivity requires a rate of increased capital-intensity, combined with an increased rate of advances in physical principles employed, which more than overcomes the rates of relative depletion. This combined function is a reflection of the role of what Academician Vernadsky defined as the Noösphere.

True economic value, is determined by consideration of the relative value defined by the functional set of relations to which I have just referred.

## Economy as a Natural Process

Actually, the rate of relative progress (after discounting for attrition) is a product of the interaction among the representatives of Vernadsky's three categories: Lithosphere, Biosphere, and Noösphere.

Contrary to all positivists and their reductionist forebears, the universe is not subject to any alleged "principle" of universal entropy. The so-called "second law of thermodynamics" is simply fraudulent, and a form of pseudo-science. The universe is anti-entropic in all respects, for each of the three categories which I have emphasized here (Lithosphere, Biosphere, and Noösphere). For what bears on the notion of the Lithosphere, the raw reflection of a principle of anti-entropy is a general succession of phases of increased anti-entropy comparable to a notion of qualitatively increasing levels of energy-flux density. Secondly, biological anti-entropy among living systems generally, is the relevant expression. Thirdly, we have the creative powers of the individual personality, as Leibniz defined "free energy" in physical terms of a principle of least action.

So, for example, living processes, by the collecting of specific arrays of minerals according to their nature, present mankind with more or less rich concentrations of what we treat as ores. Thus, in all cases, man tends to run ahead of the rate of replenishment of the relatively richest ores, which requires man to resort to modes of production of increased capital-intensity and higher rates of energy-flux density.

The array of these and related considerations, defines a physical notion of anti-entropy, which, in turn, points out the significance of the notion of higher levels of anti-entropy as the basis for the relevant notion of economic value.

## II. The Moon-Mars Mission

The progress of human society to higher levels of "anti-entropy," is marked, all along the way, by an experience fairly described as "bumping against the

V.I. Vernadsky Institute of Geochemistry, Moscow

*Vladimir I. Vernadsky and his collaborators Marie and Pierre Curie were the first scientists to understand that radioactivity would have enormous potential for the generation of energy. Vernadsky wrote in 1922: "We are approaching a great transformation in the life of mankind, with which nothing it has lived through previously can be compared. The time is not far off when man will take atomic energy into his hands, a source of power that will make it possible for him to construct his life just as he desires. This may happen in the immediate years ahead, it may happen a century from now. But it is clear that it must happen."*

upper limits" of society's progress at that time. Soon after the entry into the 20th Century, a new kind of such "upper limit" confronted us: "space travel." Albert Einstein's correction of the positivist margin of error in Hermann Minkowski's celebrated declaration, typifies this turn.

In some respects, this Twentieth-century confrontation with the challenge of space-travel was brand new. It involved the higher orders of physical processes associated with the chemistry of nuclear fission and thermonuclear fusion. In principle, it was, otherwise, a new step in a long series of steps of progress in what Academician V.I. Vernadsky was to define as the domains of the Lithosphere, Biosphere, and Noösphere, and in what might be identified as "conventional chemistries" of earlier centuries and millennia. Notably, fission and fusion were a fundamental breakthrough—off the top!—with respect to earlier forms of progress.

It was readily obvious to certain relevant Twentieth-century scientists, that the defining of the processes of fission and fusion was a qualitative breakthrough. However, what was even more important, was that these technologies implicitly defined the notion of man in space, rather than man confined to regions near to the surface of planet Earth.

Thus, man reached the Moon, but, to define that achievement properly, we must regard the Moon as the space pioneers of the last century did, as merely the essential stepping-stone to Mars. Johannes Kepler would have been gratified by that thought. The manned Moon landing brought back news of large deposits of Helium-3 isotope on the surface of the Moon;

*Space pioneer Krafft Ehricke (1917-84) wrote: "Our Moon will ... become man's cosmic front yard on which he has built super-observatories for astrophysical and stellar-planetary research, a communication center serving planetary bases, interplanetary ships and stellar vehicles, a space port for planetary and stellar vehicles, as well as hotels and hospitals."*

the prospect of relativistic flight to Mars orbit in as little as some days of transit, was now the subject. Could man withstand the combination of known and yet undefined hazards of riding in a craft traveling a highly accelerated/decelerated relativistic trajectory between the Moon and Mars-orbit? What is the exact relationship between electromagnetic and gravitational fields? How does this bear on human flight along such trajectories?

We have thus become man as functionally an inhabitant of our galaxy, on condition that we abandon the popular delusions of sense-certainty, to recognize that there is no true "empty space" within the domain of our Solar system, or the galaxy, or the universe in the very large. Thus, while we can conjecture the use of Helium-3 to power accelerated flight of some mere days' duration between Earth-orbit and Mars-orbit, we have not yet clarified the effects of such relativistic trajectories on the physical-space-time transited, effects on either the crew of the craft, or the regions of physical-space-time penetrated in this way.

Nonetheless, once we have conceptualized the challenge of such enterprises by living human beings within the Solar System, or, perhaps, our galaxy, man's conception of himself has been changed—*uplifted!*—by

sitting down to work through the questions so posed.

The most significant such consideration, at least for the present moment, is mankind's notion of physical-space-time, rather than time by itself. The significance of that is within reach of understanding, but, so far, only in a limited way, a mere, rough approximation.

The crucial issue to which such contemplations urge us to turn, involves a fundamental quality of difference between human nature and the nature of beasts. The following argument is required.

## Time & Creation

All processes in the known universe are intrinsically creative. The universe itself evolves upward in the large. The chemical composition of the Sun and its planets evolves. Living processes are characterized by upward evolution in all directions. Yet, human creativity is of a special quality. In all other systems, insofar as they are known as systems, creativity occurs without the agency of the individual will. With mankind, it is different. Actual creativity among human individuals is of a voluntary character. This quality of willfulness in human creativity is a notion comparable to the notion of a Creator of the universe.

This notion of the human individual as having access to an aspect of human nature comparable to that of a Creator, as Philo of Alexandria denounced Aristotle on this point, defines an existential quality of human creativity as such. This notion has been treated by some Christian theologians and others as expressing a concept known as "a simultaneity of eternity."

This means, that the creativity which may be expressed by an otherwise mortal form of human individual, has an ontological efficiency which permeates the successive generations engaged in a continuing creative process, a process expressed by the creative individual human mind, but a process which subsumes the creative processes of that individual human mind, or those of an entire society. Thus, on such accounts, we make a distinction between the human individual's biological existence, which is temporary, and that quality of efficient creativity which we associate not with the human body, but the soul. In other words, the

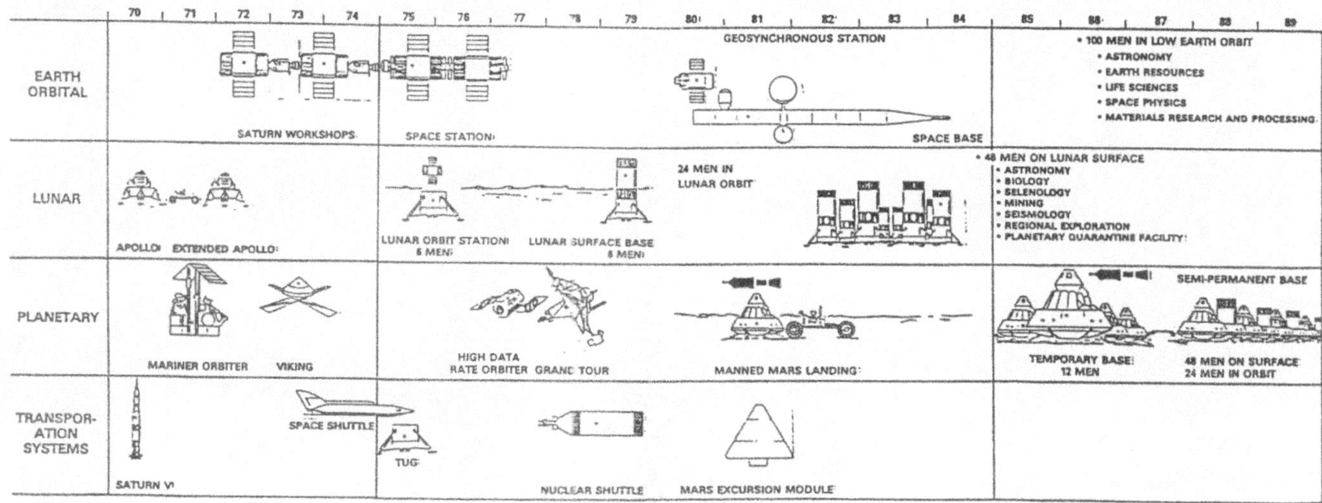


notion of the soul as an efficiently existent being dwelling within a process of universal development known as a simultaneity of eternity.

With mankind, thus, the human body is a passing expression of the essential nature of the creative powers associated with the human mind. The individual, as a creative personality, appears, thus, as an expression of a creative being, a person, who is at once both mortal and eternal in the sense of a simultaneity of the creative process with which the existence of mankind is associated in this universe.

For convenience, consider Raphael Sanzio's **The School of Athens**.

Consider each figure in that portrait. Assign the place of habitation, and dates of birth and death of each figure. Now consider the interactions among these historic figures, the interactions of ideas, as for better or for worse.

The principal lesson to be adduced is the aspects of that image of **The School of Athens** which should bear on the choice of motives of a person's sense of the purpose and meaning of the outcome of having lived one's mortal life: the notion of what one must become in the immortal outcome of living a mortal life, and living that life according to the notion of a universal principle of creativity as the distinction, the essential content, and the true purpose of a human mortal life.

It is those fears which lack of attention to the role of creativity engenders, which are the essence of evil in

*Wernher von Braun (1912-77), director of NASA's Marshall Space Flight Center, envisioned a comprehensive 20-year "Integrated Space Program, 1970-90" (shown at top). He led the development of the Saturn V booster rocket that helped land the first men on the Moon in July 1969.*

mankind. To live for the fulfilment of a creative destiny for mankind, is, ultimately, the distinction between the impulse for greedy depravity and the eternal sublime.

That is the true secret of a science of economy.